Dining In-Phoenix
COOKBOOK

TITLES IN SERIES

Dining In-Phoenix

C O O K B O O K

A Collection of Gourmet Recipes for Complete Meals from the Phoenix-Scottsdale Area's Finest Restaurants

RENEE
EAGER

Foreword by
BOB GOLDWATER

Peanut Butter Publishing
Mercer Island, Washington

Cover Photograph by Kenneth Redding
Illustrations by Neil Sweeney

ISBN 0-89716—035-5

CONTENTS

FOREWORD

There was a time not too long ago when the typical American ate pork or beef and potatoes, Italians ate pasta, and Mexicans ate a variety of tortilla-wrapped dishes. French cuisine was a rumor brought back from the wars and Chinese food meant primarily chow mein and chop suey. In those days it was nearly impossible to get fresh fish, lobster, and even the Midwest's fine corn-fed beef in Phoenix. Recent years have brought about an explosion in American tastes as well as in our capacity to transport perishables, and now our diet is among the most eclectic in the world. Italian-Americans have not given up pasta, of course, nor have Mexican-Americans forsaken tortillas—but now everyone else enjoys them too. French cooking has arrived to give body and aroma to the legends. Along with it, our interest has been captured by other, less stereotyped dishes from the many ethnic cuisines around the world, including some surprises from familiar quarters.

Because of the many people from all parts of the world who have migrated to Phoenix in particular, and because of their varied tastes and traditions, the restaurants of our city now rank among the finest in the country. Renee Eager, in *Dining In–Phoenix*, does a magnificent job of guiding us through the variety of choices they afford. The book contains a representative sampling of Phoenix's best. It is unlikely that everyone will find all of their favorites in this or any single book, but I think you will agree that the menus presented here are both inspiring and practical. The recipes, or course, are the center of attention, but equally interesting are the descriptions and histories of the restaurants and the many chefs' tips scattered throughout the book. Renee, a gourmet cook herself and, in fact, an instructor in the art, obviously enjoyed her research. I am pleased to invite you to enjoy its fruits.

Bob Goldwater

PREFACE

In a fairly short time, Phoenix has blossomed from a small town in the desert to one of the ten largest cities in the country. While it still retains some of the small-town feeling, the city's growth is evident in its expanding array of the by-products of a centralized population. Culturally oriented civic centers, symphony halls, and theaters have come to grace the city grounds; and, of course, there are the restaurants.

The restaurants in Phoenix and the neighboring cities of the Valley of the Sun are greatly influenced by the large influx of people from various parts of the country. Many people come initially for the wonderful climate and soon discover that the dining experiences in Phoenix are as varied as perhaps anywhere in the West. These expectations are reflected and fulfilled by the quality dining establishments spread throughout the valley. Likewise, the chefs' backgrounds are as varied as the city's population. Some bring with them a culinary heritage they had in their families for generations, while others are of a new fold who combine their love of fine food with a seemingly inborn creative talent. In each instance, quality pervades and the customer is the ultimate beneficiary.

In the following pages, the owners and chefs from the various restaurants featured share some of their recipes and suggestions, allowing us to create their specialties at home. The pleasure and tradition of enjoying a wonderful meal with cherished company is not confined to dining out alone. It is now possible to recreate a fine evening out at home—except, of course, for the dishes!

Since cooking is my vocation as well as avocation, compiling *Dining In– Phoenix* has truly been a rewarding experience. I would like to thank all those who cooperated with me while tolerating my never-ending questions and attempts to measure "pinches" of ingredients from one chef to the next. To all those who share in the love of fine dining—this book is for you.

Renee Eager

AMBROSINO'S ITALIAN
GOURMET DINING

Dinner for Six

Negroni Cocktails

Hot Antipasto:

Sautéed Calamari
Shrimp Française
Clams Casino
Mussels alla Marinara
Mozzarella en Carozza
Sautéed Zucchini
Stuffed Mushrooms

Tortellini al Brodo
Cold Antipasto Salad
Veal Saltimbocca alla Romana
Fettuccini di Portofino alla Ambrosino
Toasted Almond Amaretto

Beverages:

With the Veal and Fettuccini—Amarone
With the Almond Amaretto—Asti Spumante
After Dinner—Espresso and Sambuca Romana

Louis Ambrosino, Owner

Ambrosino's Italian Gourmet Dining features authentic Neapolitan and Northern Italian creations in a unique, grape-arbored villa atmosphere. A statue of Augustus Caesar, a landmark on Scottsdale Road, appears to be welcoming guests to the restaurant. Purchased from Paramount Studios, the statue previously played a part in *The Greatest Story Ever Told*. Passing the fern-draped fountain, one notices other statues, hand-carved in Guadalajara especially for the Ambrosino's, depicting six lovely Roman maidens.

Once inside, Patty Hahn greets patrons with her unending cheerfulness and bubbling personality. She delivers them into the hands of a knowledgeable and well-trained waiter, a member of a team of service personnel the *Arizona Republic* has compared to the Pope's Swiss Guard. A cocktail area holds guests awaiting tables while an efficient, pretty barmaid pours wine, serves drinks, and happily converses with everyone. The dining room has both tables and booths, candlelights, fresh linens, and an intimate atmosphere.

At any time, the kitchen doors may swing open and Louis Ambrosino may emerge from one of his periodic checks on the frenzied activity within. Warm and outgoing, he takes great enjoyment in circulating among his guests, then ducking back into the kitchen to supervise children Chris and Michael as well as the rest of the staff. (Daughter Debra helps in the dining room, assisting the hostess.) Louis is religiously dedicated to his art, a dedication that began when he was a young boy working beside his father to run a store and catering business, complete with homemade pastas and forty-five varieties of cheese, in Chicago. That store—Ambrosino's Italian and Greek Delicacies—is still in operation today, under brother Joe.

Well known for superb food made fresh to order, Ambrosino's offers a variety of dishes with origins from the mountainous Swiss border to the very tip of the Italian boot. *New Times Weekly* recently nominated Ambrosino's as the best Italian restaurant in the Valley of the Sun; it is no wonder, with all the pride and attention Louis puts into it. "I prepare my food with love and from the heart," he says.

2122 North Scottsdale Road
Scottsdale

NEGRONI COCKTAILS

1 *cup gin*	1 *cup Campari*
1 *cup sweet Italian vermouth*	6 *lemon-peel twists*

Place a dozen ice cubes in a tall pitcher. Add the gin, vermouth, and Campari. Stir and chill. Serve over ice in Old-Fashioned glasses; garnish with twists of lemon peel.

HOT ANTIPASTO

SAUTÉED CALAMARI

2 *pounds calamari*	4 *eggs, well beaten*
Peanut oil	*HOT SAUCE*
1 *cup sifted flour*	

1. Clean the calamari, removing the cranial cartilage and thin outer skins. Cut each into 3 pieces.
2. Pour the peanut oil into a deep pan to a depth of 2 inches. Heat to 325°.
3. Dust the calamari with the flour and shake off any excess. Dip in the beaten eggs. Dip in flour and eggs once more.
4. Sauté in the oil until lightly browned, about 1½ minutes. Drain on paper toweling and serve with Hot Sauce.

Take care not to overcook squid, as the flesh toughens quickly.

HOT SAUCE

1 *(8-ounce) can plum tomatoes*	⅛ *teaspoon freshly ground black pepper*
⅛ *teaspoon cracked red pepper*	⅛ *teaspoon salt*

Place ingredients in a blender and process 4 to 5 seconds.

AMBROSINO'S

SHRIMP FRANÇAISE

1 pound large (8-count) shrimp, shelled and deveined
½ cup flour
2 eggs, well beaten

Peanut Oil
1 tablespoon butter
¼ cup dry Marsala wine
½ lemon

1. Dip each shrimp in the flour, then in the beaten eggs. Repeat this procedure once more and lay the shrimp out on waxed paper.
2. Pour enough peanut oil into a sauté pan to cover the bottom. Heat over medium heat.
3. Add the shrimp and sauté slowly until golden brown. Reduce the heat and add the butter. When melted, add the Marsala. Squeeze the lemon juice over, cover, and simmer for 3 to 4 minutes.

A dash of Amaretto di Saronna may be added with the Marsala for a sweeter flavor.

CLAMS CASINO

1 sweet red pepper
1 bell pepper
½ medium-size onion
½ cup bread crumbs
¼ cup clam juice
¼ pound butter, melted

¼ cup peanut oil
Salt and pepper to taste
1 dozen fresh clams, cherrystone or littleneck
2 slices thick bacon, cut into ½" strips

1. Preheat oven to 400°.
2. Dice the peppers and onion. Thoroughly mix with the bread crumbs by hand.
3. Mix in the clam juice, butter, oil, salt, and pepper.
4. Open the clams and leave on the half-shell. Place a layer of the dressing mixture ¼" thick over each.
5. Top each clam with a piece of the bacon. Place on a baking pan and bake in preheated oven until the dressing is golden brown, about 7 to 8 minutes.

To insure the tenderness of the clams, place a small amount of water in the pan before baking, and be sure not to overcook.

MUSSELS ALLA MARINARA

2 pounds California mussels
¼ cup pure imported olive oil
¼ cup dry Chianti wine
1 (16-ounce) can imported
plum tomatoes

½ teaspoon chopped fresh
parsley
¼ teaspoon oregano

1. Thoroughly scrub the mussels under running water to remove the beards and grit.
2. In a saucepan, combine the mussels, oil, and wine with ½ cup water. Hand-crush the tomatoes into the mixture. Cover and cook over high heat for 10 to 15 minutes or until the shells open.
3. Remove to bowls with a slotted spoon, discarding any mussels that did not open. Spoon the sauce over the open mussels and sprinkle with chopped parsley and oregano.

Use California mussels rather than those from Boston—they are bigger and more easily removed from the shells.

MOZZARELLA EN CAROZZA

1 cup seasoned bread crumbs
2 teaspoons chopped parsley
1 teaspoon oregano
3 tablespoons grated
Romano cheese
1 tablespoon garlic salt
Salt and pepper to taste

1½ pounds mozzarella cheese,
cut in 2" cubes
½ cup sifted flour
3 eggs, well beaten
1 cup peanut oil

MARINARA SAUCE
(optional—see next page)

1. Combine the bread crumbs, parsley, oregano, Romano cheese, garlic salt, table salt, and pepper.
2. Dip the mozzarella cubes in the flour, then into the beaten eggs, and finally into the bread crumb mixture. Repeat this dipping procedure. Place on a sheet pan covered with waxed paper and freeze overnight.
3. Preheat oven to 400°.

(continued on next page)

4. Heat the peanut oil in a skillet over medium-high heat. Add the cheese cubes and sauté until golden brown. Remove from the pan before the cheese melts.

5. Place in a Pyrex dish. Cover with Marinara Sauce if desired. Bake in preheated oven for 6 to 7 minutes or until the cheese is soft. Serve hot.

Note: The cheese cubes may be cooked in a microwave oven for 2 minutes, rather than in a conventional oven as above.

MARINARA SAUCE

3 cloves garlic, crushed	¼ teaspoon salt
3 tablespoons olive oil	¼ teaspoon pepper
1 (16-ounce) can plum tomatoes, undrained	½ cup Chianti wine

Sauté the garlic in the olive oil over medium heat until lightly browned. Add the tomatoes and juice, salt, pepper, and wine. Simmer at least 10 minutes.

SAUTÉED ZUCCHINI

2 medium-size zucchini	2 teaspoons garlic salt
½ cup seasoned bread crumbs	⅛ teaspoon pepper
1 teaspoon chopped parsley	¼ cup sifted flour
½ teaspoon oregano	1 large egg, beaten
2 teaspoons grated Romano cheese	1 cup peanut oil

1. Slice the zucchini lengthwise in long, narrow strips, about 3" long by ½" thick.

2. Combine the bread crumbs, parsley, oregano, cheese, garlic salt, and pepper.

3. Dredge the zucchini slices in the flour. Dip in the beaten egg and coat with the bread crumb mixture. Repeat with another full layer of breading.

4. Heat the oil in a large sauté pan over medium-high heat. Rapidly sauté the zucchini strips; drain on paper toweling. Keep warm in a 300° oven or in aluminum foil until ready to serve.

STUFFED MUSHROOMS

12 large, fresh mushroom caps   Grated Parmesan cheese
⅓ pound bulk sausage

1. Preheat oven to 400°.
2. Blanch the mushroom caps in boiling water for 2 minutes to remove the rough texture. Drain and allow to cool.
3. Divide the sausage and mound in the mushroom caps. Place in a baking pan and sprinkle liberally with Parmesan cheese.
4. Bake in preheated oven for 8 to 10 minutes or until golden brown.

If the mushrooms shrink, they are overdone.

TORTELLINI AL BRODO

18 veal-stuffed tortellini   2 tablespoons Parmesan
1 quart CHICKEN STOCK   cheese
Chopped fresh parsley

1. Bring a large pot of salted water to a boil. Add the tortellini, stir, and boil until tender and doubled in size, about 15 minutes. Drain and rinse in cold water.
2. Place the Chicken Stock in a 2-quart saucepan and heat to simmering.
3. Add the drained tortellini to the broth. Allow to come back up to heat.
4. Ladle into individual bowls. Sprinkle the parsley and Parmesan cheese over.

CHICKEN STOCK

2 pounds chicken parts,   ¼ cup chopped fresh parsley
   including skin   1 bay leaf
2 carrots   ½ teaspoon salt
1 stalk celery, including tops   ¼ teaspoon white pepper
1 medium-size onion

(continued on next page)

1. Place the chicken parts in a stock pot with enough water to generously cover. Bring to a boil.
2. Chop the vegetables and add to the stock. Reduce heat to simmer.
3. Add the seasonings. Simmer 1½ hours, skimming the surface occasionally.
4. Remove the chicken parts and bay leaf. Strain the stock through a fine sieve, pushing the vegetables through for extra flavoring. Refrigerate until the fat congeals at the surface; remove fat and discard.

If you're in a hurry and don't have time to refrigerate the stock, the fat may be removed by laying strips of paper toweling over the surface of the slightly cooled stock to absorb it. This method can be messy and wasteful, and doesn't do quite as good a job, but it is indispensable in a pinch.

COLD ANTIPASTO SALAD

6 slices cappicolla ham	1 large head romaine lettuce
6 slices Genoa salami	½ cup olive oil
12 slices peperoni sausage	⅓ cup wine vinegar
3 slices prosciutto ham	Peperoncinis
3 slices mortadella sausage	Black olives
6 slices imported provolone cheese	

1. Cut the meats and cheese into ⅓"-wide juliennes.
2. Wash and dry the lettuce. Cut into 2" pieces.
3. Combine the oil and vinegar. Toss the lettuce with some of the dressing. Artfully arrange the meats, cheese, peperoncinis, and olives over the lettuce. Sprinkle with a little more of the dressing. Serve on chilled salad plates with chilled forks.

Steaming hot Italian bread with creamery butter makes an irresistible accompaniment to this salad.

VEAL SALTIMBOCCA ALLA ROMANA

3½ pounds veal steak, cut
 ½" thick
½ teaspoon crushed sage
½ teaspoon freshly ground
 black pepper
¼ pound prosciutto ham,
 sliced paper-thin

4 tablespoons butter
2 tablespoons olive or
 salad oil
3 tablespoons flour
¾ cup dry Marsala wine
 Parsley

1. Preheat oven to 325°.
2. Bone and trim the fat from the meat. Pound with a meat mallet to ⅛" thickness. Rub on one side with the sage and pepper. Cut into 4" to 5" squares.
3. Distribute the ham over the seasoned side of the veal pieces. Carefully roll up each piece and secure with wooden toothpicks.
4. Heat the butter and oil together in a large skillet over high heat. Brown the veal rolls on all sides. Remove to a 13½" by 9" by 2" baking dish, reserving the pan drippings.
5. Stir the flour into the drippings. Stir in 1½ cups water and the Marsala and bring to a boil. Pour over the veal rolls.
6. Cover the baking dish with aluminum foil and bake in preheated oven for 35 minutes or until tender. Serve garnished with parsley sprigs.

Smoked or boiled ham may be used if prosciutto is unavailable.

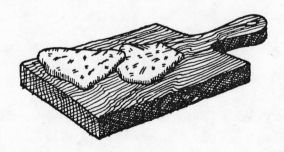

FETTUCCINI DI PORTOFINO ALLA AMBROSINO

5 ounces egg fettuccini
5 ounces spinach fettuccini
¼ pound butter
1 pint whipping cream
3 tablespoons Chicken Stock
(see index), plus more
as needed
Salt and freshly ground
black pepper to taste

¼ cup Parmesan cheese
6 medium-size mushrooms,
halved
1 cup coarsely chopped
walnuts
Grated Parmesan cheese
(optional)

1. Bring a large pot of salted water to a rolling boil. Stir in both types of noodles and cook al dente—tender, but with a faint crispness in the center. Drain.
2. Melt the butter in a saucepan and add the cream. Heat to a simmer without allowing to boil.
3. Stir in the chicken stock, salt, and pepper. Add the drained noodles and mix well.
4. Reduce the heat. Fold in the cheese; continue folding until the sauce begins to thicken. If the sauce becomes too thick, add a little more chicken stock.
5. Stir in the mushroom halves.
6. Turn out onto warmed plates. Sprinkle with the walnuts. Add a twist of pepper over each portion. Top with grated cheese if desired.

This dish should be served immediately to prevent coagulation of the sauce.

TOASTED ALMOND AMARETTO

1 quart vanilla ice cream,
    softened
1¼ cups Amaretto di
    Saronna liqueur

⅓ cup chopped almonds,
    toasted
Whipped cream

Set the ice cream at room temperature for 30 minutes or until soft enough to stir. Blend in ½ cup amaretto and the chopped almonds. Refreeze for 24 hours. When ready to serve, scoop into dessert dishes. Top each with a jigger of amaretto. Garnish with whipped cream.

We make our ice cream from scratch; if you have an ice-cream machine, I suggest you use it. Otherwise, buy the best ice cream you can find for this dessert. The quantity of chopped almonds may be altered to suit individual preference.

Dinner for Six

Antipasto di Tutto di Mare

Tortellini Portofino

Belgian Endive Avanti

Osso Buco Milanese

Sautéed Fresh Zucchini

Carote alla Catarina

Zabaglione with Strawberries

Beverages:

Apéritif—Punt e Mes, Carpano
With the Antipasto—Pinot Grìgio di Piave, 1979
With the Osso Buco—Ruffino Riserva Ducale, 1971

Angelo Livi, Franco Ferrandi, Benito Mellino,
and Ramon Vives, Owners

Raoul Penna, Jerry Guigere, and Kathleen Doeller,
Chefs de Cuisine

AVANTI

The door is graced with black silhouettes; inside, all is black, white, and greenery. In this cool, crisp atmosphere, waiters dressed to match the decor bustle about, trailing the savory aromas of an Italian kitchen among the teased and already pleased diners. Mirrored walls reflect their progress among the softly lit chrome appointments, flowers, and candles glowing on the tables.

Owners Franco Ferrandi, Angelo Livi, Benito Mellino, and Ramon Vives have each made their own sparkle a part of Avanti. "The secret is being in the business because we love it," states Franco, though he quickly adds that the key to success also lies in "dealing with only the freshest of ingredients." French, Italian, and Spanish culture join years of training and experience in Continental schools of cuisine to provide these four with a unique combination of expertise. Their experience in transforming a seventeenth-century castle on Grand Cayman Isle in the West Indies into an internationally renowned restaurant supplied additional color, as well as consolidating a few earnestly held opinions on the nature of success in the trade. "We strongly believe that only with the freshest foods available in the market, and a knowledge of taste and finesse in preparation, will our beloved friends and clientele continue to find here the things that made it enticing in the first place," Franco says.

This approach may seem conservative, and indeed it is, in the best sense of the term. But "avanti" means "forward", and the four strive to live up to the name. They continue to travel to Europe and elsewhere, combing the cities and countryside for new and unique ideas to bring back with them. Once returned, they have an able staff of chefs—both European and American—to adapt new recipes or improve old ones. The owners themselves alternate between the Phoenix and Scottsdale locations, supervising the preparation and the attentive, friendly service of identical menus at the two restaurants, which have already garnered many culinary awards.

2728 Thomas Road, Phoenix
3102 North Scottsdale Road, Scottsdale

ANTIPASTO DI TUTTO DI MARE

1 medium-size squid (calamari)	6 peppercorns
¼ pound butter	1 bay leaf
½ cup plus 2 tablespoons white wine	1½ cups clam juice
1 cup red wine	24 fresh mussels, well scrubbed
3 tablespoons baking soda	12 large, pitted black olives
1 pound octopus	MARINADE (see next page)
1 large russet potato	2 heads butter lettuce
12 large shrimp	3 tomatoes
2 lemons	Parsley sprigs

1. Bring enough water to amply cover the squid to a boil in a medium pot. Separate the head from the tentacles. Remove the transparent outer skin, ink sac, and cartilage. Boil the head and tentacles for 2 hours.

2. Drain the squid and cut into 2" pieces. Melt the butter in a sauté pan over medium heat. Add the squid and sauté until tender, about 6 minutes, adding ¼ cup white wine a little at a time as the butter reduces. When the squid is tender, remove from heat and drain.

3. In a 6-quart pot, bring 4 quarts water, the red wine, and baking soda to a boil. Add the octopus and boil 1 hour.

4. Drain the octopus. Remove the outer skin; it should slip off easily. Cut the meat into bite-size pieces.

5. Peel the potato. Boil whole just until cooked through, about 20 minutes. Drain and allow to cool. Cut in ¼" by ½" dice.

6. Shell the shrimp; devein and rinse. Bring water to a boil in a 1-quart pot.

7. Cut 1 lemon in half lengthwise; cut one half in two and squeeze the juice into the water. Add the peppercorns, bay leaf, and shrimp. Boil 3 minutes, drain, and place in ice water.

8. Place the clam juice and remaining white wine in a large pan. Add the mussels, cover, and steam until the shells are wide open. Remove from heat, discarding any unopened mussels, and place the rest in ice water.

(continued on next page)

9. Cut the shrimp into ½" pieces. Slice the olives into ⅛"-thick rings. Shell the mussels, reserving the shells intact.

10. Combine the octopus, squid, shrimp, mussels, potato, and olives in a stainless-steel bowl. Add the Marinade. Cover with plastic wrap and refrigerate at least 2½ hours.

11. Line 6 chilled salad plates with the lettuce. Place a heaping mound of the marinated seafood in the center of each. Cut the remaining 1½ lemons into 12 wedges. Garnish each plate with 2 lemon wedges, 3 tomato wedges, 3 mussel shells, and a bouquet of fresh parsley sprigs.

MARINADE

1 *tablespoon finely chopped*
   fresh parsley
2 *lemons*
6 *large cloves garlic, peeled*

½ *cup Bertolli olive oil*
2 *tablespoons chopped*
   pimiento

1. Place the parsley in a clean cloth. Wrap tightly and wash under running water. Wring the cloth to squeeze out the moisture.

2. Squeeze the juice of the lemons into a bowl, removing seeds.

3. Mince the garlic extremely finely. Add to the lemon juice.

4. Add the parsley, olive oil, and chopped pimiento. Mix well.

TORTELLINI PORTOFINO

1 tablespoon salt	1¾ cups whipping cream
1 pound frozen tortellini	⅓ cup chopped walnuts
10 large mushroom caps	1 cup freshly grated
4 tablespoons butter	Parmesan cheese
2 egg yolks	Freshly ground black pepper

1. Place 4 quarts water with the salt in a large pot. Bring to a boil and stir in the tortellini, cooking until the pasta rises to the surface and is al dente. Drain and rinse under cool running water.
2. Slice the mushroom caps ¼" thick. Melt the butter in a sauté pan over medium-high heat and sauté until tender. Drain on paper toweling.
3. Whip the egg yolks with ¼ cup whipping cream. Set aside.
4. Heat the remaining 1½ cups cream in a 10" sauté pan. When bubbles begin to form around the edge, add the mushrooms and chopped walnuts. Allow to heat through.
5. Quickly reheat the tortellini by submerging in boiling water to cover. Drain and add to the simmering cream. Toss to coat well.
6. Add the Parmesan cheese a little at a time, tossing constantly until melted.
7. Mix in the reserved egg yolk/cream mixture. Toss again and divide among 6 shallow bowls. Finish with a few twists of black pepper.

BELGIAN ENDIVE AVANTI

4 medium-size heads Belgian endive	2 medium-size firm tomatoes
4 heads green Kentucky Bibb lettuce	2 Red Delicious apples
	DRESSING
	6 sprigs fresh mint

1. Slice the endives on the bias about ½" apart. Refrigerate.
2. Core the lettuce. Wash the leaves individually under cold running water. Drain and refrigerate.
3. Core the tomatoes and blanch 1 minute in boiling water. Remove with a slotted spoon. Peel and cut into 6 wedges each.
4. Core the apples and slice into paper-thin sections. Place in the Dressing and stir gently to coat.
5. Place the endive in a salad bowl. Holding a knife or spatula against the bowl of Dressing to retain the apples, pour the Dressing over the endive. Toss gently but thoroughly with 2 spoons.
6. Line individual salad plates with the outer leaves of the lettuce. Place the hearts over. Arrange the endive around the lettuce hearts. Arrange the apple slices over. Garnish with tomato wedges and mint sprigs.

DRESSING

1 tablespoon chopped fresh parsley	3 cloves garlic, minced
2 tablespoons Bertolli olive oil	3 fresh shallots, minced
¼ cup walnut oil	1 tablespoon granulated sugar
¼ cup wine vinegar	¼ cup shelled pecan halves
2 tablespoons Grey Poupon mustard	

1. Place the parsley in a clean cloth and wash under cool running water. Squeeze tightly to extract the moisture.
2. Combine the olive oil, walnut oil, vinegar, and mustard in a bowl, whisking vigorously. Whisk in the parsley, garlic, shallots, and sugar. Add the pecans.

OSSO BUCO MILANESE

1½ cups flour	2 shallots, minced
Salt and freshly ground black pepper to taste	1 clove garlic, minced
	½ teaspoon thyme
6 veal shanks, on the bone	1 teaspoon fresh tarragon
¾ cup plus 2 tablespoons Bertolli olive oil	2 bay leaves
	¼ cup chopped fresh parsley
2 medium-size white onions, chopped	½ cup dry white wine
	1½ cups veal stock
2 stalks celery, sliced ¼"	5 to 6 tomatoes
7 carrots, peeled and sliced ¼"	RICE (see next page)

1. Preheat oven to 375°.
2. Season the flour with salt and black pepper. Dredge the veal shanks in the flour, shaking off the excess.
3. Heat 6 tablespoons olive oil until very hot in a large, heavy pan. Sear the veal shanks in the hot oil, turning to brown all sides. Do not allow to burn.
4. Heat the remaining ½ cup oil in a Dutch oven or roasting pan. Sauté the onions, celery, carrots, shallots, and garlic until the onions are translucent. Add the thyme, tarragon, bay leaves, and parsley.
5. Place the browned veal shanks over the vegetables. Add the wine and half the veal stock. Boil uncovered over high heat until the liquid is reduced to one-third of its original volume.
6. Core the tomatoes and blanch in boiling water for 1 minute. Peel, seed, and coarsely chop. When the veal liquid has been reduced, add the tomatoes, remaining veal stock, and salt and pepper to taste. Cover the pan and bake 1½ to 2 hours, or until the veal is extremely tender and the sauce is glossy and thick. Check periodically to see that there is still liquid in the pan. If necessary, add more veal stock and as much as ⅓ cup more wine.
7. Serve over Rice, with plenty of sauce and vegetables.

RICE

¼ cup Bertolli olive oil	1½ cups white rice
1 medium-size white onion, minced	3 cups Chicken Stock (see index), warm
1 stalk celery, diced	⅛ teaspoon saffron
1 clove garlic, minced	⅛ teaspoon salt

1. Heat the olive oil in a 2-quart pot. Add the onion, celery, and garlic and sauté until translucent. Add the rice and sauté, stirring constantly, until a nutty aroma is evident. Do not allow to burn.
2. Add the chicken stock, saffron, and salt. Reduce heat and simmer until all the liquid is absorbed and the rice is tender, about 20 minutes.
3. Remove from heat. Let stand, covered, until dry and fluffy.

SAUTÉED FRESH ZUCCHINI

3 medium-size zucchini	¼ cup clarified butter
2 sprigs fresh basil	⅛ teaspoon salt

1. Wash the zucchini and remove the ends. Slice lengthwise in half; slice the halves crosswise ¼" thick.
2. Wash the basil. Discard the stems and coarsely chop the leaves.
3. Heat the clarified butter in a sauté pan over medium-high heat. Add the basil and salt and sauté briefly.
4. Add the zucchini and sauté until tender but not limp. Remove with a slotted spoon.

Note: To clarify butter, melt it in a narrow pot. Skim the foam, pour off the clear liquid, and discard the solids left in the bottom of the pot.

CAROTE ALLA CATARINA

4 carrots, peeled
Salt
3 tablespoons clarified butter
2 tablespoons orange-
blossom honey

2 teaspoons crushed fresh
tarragon
2 tablespoons ginger ale

1. Remove the tops and heels from the carrots. Cut into matchsticks about 1½" by ¼ inch.
2. Bring 1 quart water and 2 teaspoons salt to a boil. Add the carrot sticks and cook until crisp-tender. Drain and place under cold running water. Drain again.
3. Heat the butter in a sauté pan. Add ⅛ teaspoon salt and the honey. When the honey has melted, add the carrots and tarragon. Toss and stir until piping hot.
4. Add the ginger ale. Toss and stir.

ZABAGLIONE WITH STRAWBERRIES

8 medium egg yolks
6 tablespoons granulated
sugar
⅔ cup Marsala wine

24 medium-size fresh
strawberries
6 fresh mint sprigs

1. Place the egg yolks in a stainless steel or copper bowl. Whisk vigorously, gradually adding the sugar and Marsala.
2. Place the bowl over a pot of simmering water. (The water should not touch the bottom of the bowl.) Continue whisking until a thick, light-yellow custard develops. When the custard begins to pull away from the bottom of the bowl, remove from heat.
3. Reserve 6 choice strawberries; slice the remainder and place in 6 stemmed wine glasses. Pour the custard over and garnish with the reserved strawberries and the mint sprigs. Serve warm or refrigerate before serving.

The Chaparral

Dinner for Four

Soupe de Saumon à la Crème

Coeurs de Romaine Maison

Cuisses de Grenouilles Provençale

Strawberry Sorbet

Carré d'Agneau en Croûte à ma Façon

Bouquetière de Légumes

Notre Soufflé au Chocolat

Wines:

With the Soup—Pouilly-Fuissé, Louis Jadot

With the Lamb—Château Talbot, St.-Julien, or a Moulin à Vent, Beaujolais

Jean Paul Ybry, Sous-Chef

CHAPARRAL ROOM

When the Camelback Inn first opened in 1936, Phoenix residents drove a long, dusty trail to enjoy meals in its small dining room way out in Scottsdale. There were few good restaurants around in those days, but one could always count on an impressive meal at the Inn. Since then the Phoenix-Scottsdale area, as the hub of the sunbelt explosion, has grown both in population and in dining sophistication. Still, some things remain the same.

The beautiful old inn, acquired by the Marriott Corporation in 1967, continues to be known as one of those special places for quality dining. It has won virtually every hospitality and dining award, including the *Mobil Travel Guide's* Five Star Award, and the American Automobile Association's Five Diamond Award. Word has obviously spread about the attention to detail in evidence here, including such extras as cakes, pastries, and breads—even hamburger and hot dog buns—being made on the premises. Martha Kain, a former farm woman now in her seventies, supervises the bakery department; her family recipes are now the standard for the entire ninety-plus chain.

Among the coffee shops and lavish poolside buffets, the Chaparral Room is the Inn's specialty restaurant. Decorated in red and black with pleasant pink accents, the Chaparral Room is impressive in its utilization of Southwest themes in the decor. Large, artfully arranged brass planters brim with bright red silk flowers. Attentive tableside service, a nicely balanced wine list, and, of course, Continental cuisine prepared from the freshest of ingredients add up to an evening to remember.

"We aren't afraid to be creative with the classic ways of cooking," says Executive Chef Franz Ferschke (whose passion when not cooking is pyramids—he has made it a lifetime goal to see them all, from the Yucatan to Giza). "Nouvelle cuisine is one of those overused phrases, but I will say that we don't cover up the food; we rarely sauce vegetables, for example, preferring to use herbs and spices to bring out their flavor." Lobster Bisque, Flamed Spinach Salad, individual racks of lamb, Scampi Biscay, and Grand Marnier Soufflé are favored by the Chaparral Room clientele, which includes many names from the worlds of politics and entertainment. A VIP menu, available to groups of ten or more on a special-order basis, is also featured.

Marriott's Camelback Inn
Lincoln Drive
Scottsdale

SOUPE DE SAUMON A LA CRÈME
Creamy Salmon Soup

1 quart *FISH STOCK*
¼ pound salmon, diced

½ cup whipping cream
Fresh chopped dill

1. Bring the Fish Stock to a boil.
2. Reduce heat and add the salmon. Simmer 5 minutes.
3. Remove from heat. Gently stir in the cream. Place in a soup tureen or individual bowls. Sprinkle with dill.

FISH STOCK

½ onion, diced
1 stalk celery, diced
1 cup white wine
1 pound bones of white-fleshed fish

1 quart water
3 black peppercorns
½ bay leaf
3 sprigs parsley

Simmer all ingredients for approximately 45 minutes. Strain through cheesecloth.

COEURS DE ROMAINE MAISON
Hearts of Romaine, House Dressing

2 hearts romaine lettuce
1 tomato, cut in wedges

4 fresh mushrooms, sliced
DRESSING

Cut the romaine hearts in half. Arrange on chilled salad plates. Garnish with tomato wedges and sliced mushrooms. Drizzle with Dressing.

DRESSING

¼ cup red wine vinegar
2 tablespoons Grey Poupon mustard

Salt and pepper to taste
¾ cup salad oil

Thoroughly mix the vinegar, mustard, and salt and pepper. Vigorously whisk in the salad oil.

CUISSES DE GRENOUILLES PROVENÇALE
Sautéed Frog Legs Provençale

24 *small frogs' legs*
Flour for dredging
¾ *pound butter*
1 *tablespoon chopped garlic*

2 *tomatoes, chopped*
2 *tablespoons chopped parsley*
  plus more for garnish
Salt and pepper to taste

1. Dredge the frogs' legs in flour. Sauté in oil over medium-high heat for 3 to 5 minutes or until cooked. Set on a serving platter; keep warm.
2. Melt the butter in a sauté pan. Add the garlic and sauté until tender. Add the tomatoes, 2 tablespoons parsley, salt, and pepper and simmer 1 minute.
3. Pour the sauce over the frog legs. Garnish with chopped parsley.

STRAWBERRY SORBET

⅓ *cup sugar*
⅓ *cup water*
1½ *pints fresh, ripe*
  strawberries, hulled

1 *tablespoon Grand Marnier*
1 *tablespoon orange juice*

1. Combine the sugar and water in a saucepan over medium heat and stir until the sugar is dissolved. Remove from heat.
2. Reserve 4 large strawberries for garnish. Place the remainder in a blender or food processor and process until puréed. Add the Grand Marnier and orange juice. Process until blended.
3. Add the sugar syrup and blend.
4. Transfer to ice-cube trays and freeze at least 12 hours.
5. When well frozen, process in a blender to a snowy consistency. Return to the freezer until ready to serve. Serve one small scoop per person, garnished with the reserved strawberries.

CARRÉ D'AGNEAU EN CROÛTE A MA FAÇON
Stuffed Rack of Lamb in Baked Crust

4 (¾ to 1-pound) racks
   of lamb
5 tablespoons butter
1 pound fresh mushrooms,
   finely diced
2 shallots, finely chopped

Salt and pepper to taste
6 ounces Puff Pastry Dough
   (see index)
1 egg
1 tablespoon milk
MADEIRA SAUCE

1. Bone the lamb racks. Trim off any fat and membranous tissue.
2. Melt 4 tablespoons butter in a large sauté pan over high heat. Add the lamb racks and sear on all sides until browned. Remove from heat and refrigerate until cool.
3. Melt the remaining butter and sauté the mushrooms and shallots until tender. Season with salt and pepper and allow to cool.
4. Preheat oven to 375°.
5. Spread the mushroom mixture over the cooled lamb racks. Roll out the puff pastry dough very thinly. Cut into pieces ample enough to wrap the racks. Beat the egg and milk together and brush the dough with the mixture. Wrap the racks and brush again with egg wash, taking care to seal the edges with the wash.
6. Bake in preheated oven for 15 minutes or until nicely browned. Serve with Madeira Sauce in sauceboats.

MADEIRA SAUCE

2 shallots, chopped
1 tablespoon butter
3 cups brown sauce

Salt and pepper to taste
½ cup Madeira wine

Sauté the shallots in the butter until tender. Stir in the brown sauce and simmer 15 minutes. Season to taste with salt and pepper and remove from heat. Stir in the wine before serving.

Brown sauce may be prepared at home, using beef drippings, or may be purchased at specialty stores and many groceries.

BOUQUETIÈRE DE LÉGUMES
Bouquet of Vegetables

16 *medium-size asparagus*
   spears
1 *cup green peas*
1 *medium-size zucchini,*
   sliced
3 *tablespoons butter*

2 *tomatoes, halved*
1 *cup seasoned bread crumbs*
4 *canned artichoke bottoms*
   Salt and pepper

1. Steam the asparagus and green peas for 5 minutes or until al dente. Remove and drain.
2. Sauté the zucchini in the butter over medium-high heat for 3 minutes or until al dente. Remove from heat.
3. Sprinkle the cut surfaces of the tomato halves with the bread crumbs. Place under a heated broiler for 1 minute or until heated through.
4. To serve, place the artichoke bottoms on 4 plates. Place the peas in the bottoms. Arrange the remaining vegetables around in an appetizing fashion. Season to taste with salt and pepper.

NOTRE SOUFFLÉ AU CHOCOLAT
Chapparal Chocolate Soufflé

¼ cup brewed coffee
1¼ cups half-and-half
6 ounces semisweet chocolate,
 cut into small chunks
3 tablespoons butter
¼ cup flour

4 egg yolks
¼ cup sugar
¼ teaspoon salt
6 egg whites
¼ teaspoon cream of tartar

1. Heat the coffee and half-and-half almost to a boil. Remove from heat and stir in the chocolate until melted.
2. Heat the butter to bubbling. Stir in the flour thoroughly. Remove from heat and add the chocolate mixture, stirring well.
3. Beat the egg yolks with 3 tablespoons sugar and the salt until light. Stir into the chocolate mixture. Set aside until cool.
4. Preheat oven to 400°.
5. Beat the egg whites with the cream of tartar until soft peaks form. Add the remaining 1 tablespoon sugar and beat until incorporated.
6. Fold the egg whites into the cooled chocolate mixture.
7. Prepare 4 individual soufflé cups by buttering the bottoms and sides, then swishing 1 teaspoon granulated sugar in each. Pour out any excess sugar. Place the batter in the cups and bake in preheated oven for 25 to 30 minutes, or until well puffed and lightly browned. Serve immediately.

CHEZ LOUIS

Dinner for Six

Saumon Poché, Sauce Mousseline

Crème de Monaco

Suprême de Faisan Paysanne

Wild Rice

Salade du Jardin

Coupe Belle Epoque

Beverages:

With the Saumon Poché—Château Olivier, white Graves

With the Faisan—Beaune, Clos des Ursules, Louis Jadot

With the Coupe—a vintage Port

After Dinner—French-roast coffee

Louis Germain, Owner and Chef

CHEZ LOUIS

Tucked away among the greenery and sculptures of Scottsdale's Civic Center Plaza, Chez Louis has enjoyed a reputation for fine dining in tasteful surroundings since 1958. As soon as one encounters the eight-foot arrangement of silk flowers in the foyer, one is struck with the restaurant's elegance. Lavender, crimson, and recessed lighting define the bar. The three dining areas are decorated in complementary themes: the Front Room, in salmon and silver, with circular black booths and cane-back chairs; the Parrot Room or Green Room, named alternately for the large green bird on the central light fixture or for its lush greenery, set off by white wicker furniture; and the Patio Room, with its glass-enclosed view of the Civic Center gardens. Mirrored columns, hand painted with vines and flowers, help to unite the themes.

Most of the baking is done by proprietor Louis Germain, who starts his working day while most of us are still asleep. Homemade rolls, breads, and pastries are served to diners and sold in the outdoor pantry—an extension of the restaurant at which cheese, wines, and other goods may also be purchased. Monsieur Germain's career began at the age of fifteen, when he started an apprenticeship at the first of several internationally known restaurants. Here he gathered the knowledge of cooking and management that have enabled him to indulge in several fancies, from creating new dishes such as the popular Oeufs à la Chez Louis—poached eggs on artichoke bottoms, dressed with Hollandaise sauce—to raising Arabian horses, photographs of which grace one wall of Chez Louis.

In addition to regular lunch and dinner service and private banquet facilities, Monsieur Germain has instituted another very special service, known as "le cercle de lundi"—"the Monday Club." On the first Monday evening of each winter month, he prepares an elaborate meal from the myriad themes of French cuisine. Intended for those who are familiar with the grand pleasures of the French table as well as for those who wish to be, these dinners are open to the general public—though reservations are recommended.

Civic Center Plaza
Scottsdale

CHEZ LOUIS

SAUMON POCHÉ, SAUCE MOUSSELINE

1 small salmon, or 1 large
   salmon tail
1 carrot, chopped
1 stalk celery, chopped

1 onion, chopped
Several sprigs of parsley
SAUCE MOUSSELINE

1. Wrap the salmon in cheesecloth. Place in a pan with the carrot, celery, onion, parsley, and water to cover. Bring to a boil and poach until the fish flakes easily with a fork. Remove from heat; let cool in the poaching liquid.
2. Remove the salmon from the broth and remove the cheesecloth. Divide the meat into 6 portions. Serve with Sauce Mousseline.

The salmon gains additional flavor if left in the broth to cool.

SAUCE MOUSSELINE

1 teaspoon crushed black
   pepper
3 shallots, chopped
2 tablespoons white vinegar
3 egg yolks

1 cup plus 2 tablespoons
   clarified butter, warm
Salt and pepper to taste
Juice of 1 lemon
½ cup stiffly whipped cream

1. Heat the pepper and shallots in the vinegar until the liquid has evaporated. Transfer to the top of a double boiler over simmering water.
2. Add the egg yolks one at a time, whisking vigorously. Add 7 tablespoons water, one at a time. Whisk until the consistency is that of thick cream. Remove from heat and allow to cool slightly.
3. When the bowl is cool enough to hold in your palm, whisk in the warm butter. Season to taste with salt and pepper.
4. Whisk in the lemon juice, then fold in the whipped cream.

Mousseline is a variation of Hollandaise sauce. To make it the standard way, fold 3 tablespoons of whipped cream into 1 cup Hollandaise.

CRÈME DE MONACO

1 quart Chicken Stock (see
   index)
½ cup diced onion
6 tablespoons butter

6 tablespoons flour
2 bunches watercress
1 cup light cream
Salt and pepper to taste

1. Bring the stock to a boil. Add the onion and simmer 30 minutes.
2. Melt the butter over medium heat. Stir in the flour to make a roux. Cook, stirring constantly, for 5 minutes. Do not allow to brown.
3. Remove the leaves of the watercress and reserve. Chop the stems and add to the stock.
4. Gradually spoon the stock into the roux, stirring until thickened and smooth.
5. Bring to a boil, then reduce heat to a bare simmer. Heat the cream separately and add to the stock. Season with salt and pepper. Garnish with the reserved watercress leaves.

This soup may be prepared ahead of time and reheated, but it does not freeze well.

CHEZ LOUIS

SUPRÊME DE FAISAN PAYSANNE

2 carrots, chopped
1 onion, chopped
1 stalk celery, chopped
1 large potato, chopped
1 turnip, chopped

3 strips bacon
¼ cup oil
6 pheasant breasts, boned
½ cup white wine

1. Preheat oven to 350°.
2. Parboil the carrots, onion, celery, potato, and turnip about 5 minutes. Drain.
3. Fry the bacon until almost crisp. Drain all but about 2 tablespoons of the fat. Add the parboiled vegetables and sauté about 3 minutes, or until heated through.
4. In a separate pan, heat the oil over medium-high heat. Add the pheasant breasts and sauté until lightly browned. Remove the pheasant to a casserole. Drain the oil from the pan and deglaze with the wine.
5. Add the sautéed vegetables to the pheasant in the casserole. Pour the pan sauce over. Cover and bake in preheated oven for 25 to 30 minutes. Serve the pheasant with the vegetables sprinkled over.

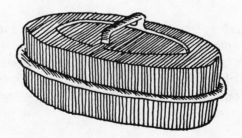

WILD RICE

1 cup wild rice	¼ cup butter
BOUQUET GARNI	4 chicken livers
Salt and pepper	½ cup chopped onions
Nutmeg	

1. Wash the rice in cold water until the water runs clear. Cover with fresh water and soak 30 minutes. Drain well.
2. Place the rice in a 2-quart pan and pour 3 cups boiling water over. Add the Bouquet Garni and salt, pepper, and nutmeg to taste. Simmer, covered, for 35 minutes.
3. In a separate pan, melt the butter over medium-high heat. Add the chicken livers and onion and sauté until the livers are cooked, about 8 minutes.
4. When the rice is cooked, remove the Bouquet Garni. Stir in the livers and onion, and serve immediately.

BOUQUET GARNI

1 bay leaf	1 sprig thyme
6 sprigs parsley	2 sprigs celery leaf

Place on a small square of cheesecloth. Tie securely with thread.

SALADE DU JARDIN

¼ head iceberg lettuce	⅓ cup wine vinegar
¼ head romaine	⅔ cup light salad oil
¼ head escarole	1 teaspoon Dijon mustard
¼ head Belgian endive	Pinch of oregano
1 small bunch watercress, leaves only	Salt and pepper to taste

Wash the greens well and tear into bite-size pieces. Combine in a bowl. Combine the remaining ingredients, mixing thoroughly. Pour over the greens and serve on chilled salad plates.

COUPE BELLE ÉPOQUE

1 *quart vanilla ice cream*	6 *MERINGUE ROUNDS*
3 *ounces orange-flavored liqueur*	*CHESTNUT CREME*

1. Allow the ice cream to soften about 20 minutes at room temperature. Blend the liqueur through and return to freezer until ready to use.
2. Scoop the ice cream into six dessert dishes. Place a Meringue Round over each. Place the Chestnut Creme in a pastry bag and pipe around the edges of the dishes in an attractive design. Re-freeze until ready to serve.

MERINGUE ROUNDS

5 *egg whites*	1 *cup sugar*

Preheat oven to 150°. Beat the egg whites until soft peaks form. Gradually add the sugar while continuing to beat to stiff peaks. Prepare a baking sheet by covering with parchment or brown paper. Place the meringue in 2″ dollops on the paper and bake 4 hours in preheated oven.

CHESTNUT CREME

¼ *pound butter*	2 *tablespoons kirsch*
6 *ounces canned candied chestnuts (marrons glacées)*	

Combine and whip well.

EL CHORRO LODGE

Dinner for Four

Consommé Bellevue

Heart of Romaine with Avocado and Grapefruit,
Lemon-Honey Dressing

Alaskan King Crabmeat Stroganoff

Fresh Green Beans au Beurre

Chocolate Ice-Box Cake

Wine:

Zeller Schwartz Katz

Joe and Evie Miller, Owners

Bill Warren, Chef

EL CHORRO LODGE

El Chorro Lodge has been a landmark since 1937, when Mark Gruber converted a private girls' school into an attractive resort. Now owned by two former employees of twenty years, Joe and Evie Miller, the Lodge offers "just plain American food" in a rustic atmosphere of beamed ceilings, fireplaces, and optional patio dining overlooking mountains and desert. Indian artwork adorns the walls and copper highlights the furnishings, from the fireplace hood and a substantial custom-made chandelier to the many planters and even the fittings on the glass room dividers. The fireplaces enhance the night air with the scent of burning mesquite, over which the aromas of the kitchen play tantalizingly.

"We start with the best-quality foodstuffs available," says Joe. "We cook them to order, and what you get is good food." At El Chorro Lodge, nothing is made ahead except the famous Sticky Buns which are served with breakfast, lunch, and dinner. "We make about two thousand every day. Most guests take some home to enjoy the next day. They're the type Grandma used to make—very rich, but boy are they good!" Other specialties include Shad Roe on Toast, Rocky Mountain Trout Amandine, Chateaubriand, and Pan-Fried Chicken. Since everything is cooked to order, some items may take a little longer than one is used to. If the Pan-Fried Chicken is ordered, for example, Joe suggests a drink on the patio in the cooling evening air while waiting.

5550 Lincoln Drive
Scottsdale

CONSOMMÉ BELLEVUE

2 cups Chicken Stock (see
    index)
2 cups clam juice

5 egg whites
¼ cup unsweetened whipped
    cream

Place the chicken stock and clam juice in a pot. Add the egg whites and bring to a boil. Cook until the egg whites have risen to the surface. Remove from heat and strain through cheesecloth. Ladle into heated soup cups and top each with a tablespoon of whipped cream.

The egg whites are used to clarify the broth.

HEART OF ROMAINE WITH AVOCADO AND GRAPEFRUIT,
Lemon-Honey Dressing

1 head romaine lettuce
1 pink grapefruit

2 avocados
LEMON-HONEY DRESSING

1. Wash and drain the lettuce. Reserve several of the large outer leaves; cut the remaining head in quarters.
2. Peel and section the grapefruit.
3. Split the avocados in half. Remove the pits and peel. Slice.
4. Line a salad plate or bowl with the reserved romaine leaves. Place the quartered heart over. Alternate grapefruit sections and avocado slices around. Drizzle the dressing over.

LEMON-HONEY DRESSING

Juice of 2 lemons
¼ teaspoon dry mustard
2 tablespoons strained honey

½ cup salad oil
Salt and pepper to taste

Thoroughly combine all ingredients. Chill before using.

ALASKAN KING CRABMEAT STROGANOFF

1 small white onion,
    finely diced
½ pound mushrooms, sliced
1 tablespoon butter
1 pound Alaskan king
    crabmeat
¼ cup white wine

3 tablespoons ketchup
2 teaspoons Worcestershire
    sauce
3 cups CREAM SAUCE
Salt and pepper
¼ cup sour cream
Cooked egg noodles

1. Sauté the onions and mushrooms in the butter until tender.
2. Add the crabmeat and wine. Reduce heat and simmer a few minutes.
3. Add the ketchup, Worcestershire sauce, and Cream Sauce and simmer to heat through. Taste for seasoning and adjust with salt and pepper.
4. Fold in the sour cream. Allow to heat.
5. Serve on beds of noodles.

CREAM SAUCE

3 tablespoons butter
3 tablespoons flour

3 cups light cream

1. Melt the butter over medium-high heat. Add the flour and cook, stirring constantly, for 5 minutes. Do not allow to brown.
2. Add the cream. Stir until the mixture is bubbly and of a batter-like consistency.

FRESH GREEN BEANS AU BEURRE

1 pound firm, fresh green
   beans
⅛ teaspoon baking soda

¼ pound butter
Salt and pepper

1. Snap the ends off the beans. Wash and drain well.
2. Place in a pan and cover with cold water. Stir in the baking soda. Bring to a boil and cook until the beans are tender. Drain off any remaining water.
3. Separately, melt the butter and brown lightly. Stir into the beans. Season to taste with salt and pepper.

CHOCOLATE ICE-BOX CAKE

¼ pound German sweet
   chocolate
2 egg yolks
1½ teaspoons confectioners'
   sugar
¼ cup chopped walnuts

1 egg white
¼ cup whipping cream, plus
   more for garnish
1 dozen ladyfingers, split

1. Melt the chocolate in the top of a double boiler over simmering water. Blend in 1 tablespoon water.
2. Remove from heat and beat in the egg yolks, one at a time, until smoothly blended.
3. Add the sugar and walnuts. Mix well.
4. Beat the egg white until stiff. Gently fold into the chocolate mixture.
5. Whip the cream until stiff. Fold into the chocolate mixture.
6. Line a 1½-quart Pyrex dish or loaf pan with the split ladyfingers. Pour in the chocolate mixture. Refrigerate 12 to 24 hours. Serve with additional whipped cream.

At El Chorro we make the Ice-Box Cake with French sponge cake, but ladyfingers are much more convenient for the home kitchen.

Dinner for Four

Demetri's Paglia e Fieno

Prawns in Garlic with Dry Spanish Sherry

Salad Conde de Orgaz

Filet of Sole Sabbagh

Flán

Demetri Velasco, Owner

DEMETRI'S

The atmosphere at Demetri's is one of muted elegance. The dining rooms are softly lit, the deep blue of the upholstery and the pink tablecloths set off by silk flowers, potted plants, mirrors, and chrome. Quiet music filters through the several rooms to enhance a sense of privacy and, perhaps, romance. Seating has been limited to sixty, a fact which makes reservations mandatory at this popular establishment.

Owner and chef Demetri Velasco hails from Spain; his culinary career began at the age of twelve with an apprenticeship at an uncle's restaurant. Then he was on to the Ritz Hotel in Madrid, private employment with a family of royalty in London, then Venezuela, finally arriving in New York with occupation listed as "restaurant specialist." There he was employed at the Waldorf Astoria, the Four Seasons, and the Marco Polo Club, among other establishments of note.

Demetri strives for quality food, prepared fresh and served simply. The cuisine is truly Continental with an accent on the sunny south, and particularly the Mediterranean cooking of Italy and Spain.

4302 North Scottsdale Road
Scottsdale

DEMETRI'S PAGLIA E FIENO
Straw and Hay

¼ *pound thin white egg*
  noodles
¼ *pound thin green egg*
  noodles
1 *quart whipping cream*
¼ *pound butter*
2 *egg yolks*

1 *cup grated Swiss cheese*
¼ *pound prosciutto ham,*
  julienned
1 *cup grated Parmesan*
  cheese
Freshly ground black
pepper

1. Place both pastas in ample boiling salted water and cook for 2½ minutes. Drain.
2. Heat the cream in a sauté pan. Add the butter in pats; stir until melted. Stir in the egg yolks, then the Swiss cheese, and finally the prosciutto.
3. Mix in the drained noodles. Remove from heat.
4. Stir in the Parmesan cheese and pepper to taste. Serve immediately.

The combination of the two cheeses, the two noodles, and the prosciutto result in an attractive dish which teases the palate.

PRAWNS IN GARLIC WITH DRY SPANISH SHERRY

8 *large prawns*
6 *tablespoons butter*
6 *tablespoons oil*
1 *teaspoon chopped fresh*
  garlic

⅛ *teaspoon crushed red pepper*
8 *large mushrooms,*
  quartered
¼ *cup dry Spanish sherry*
¼ *cup chicken consommé*

1. Shell and devein the prawns. Slice into bite-size pieces.
2. Heat the butter and oil together in a large pan over medium-high heat. Add the garlic, red pepper, mushrooms, and prawns. Sauté 1 minute.
3. Add the sherry and chicken consommé; sauté 3 minutes more. Serve in individual ramekins.

Hot French bread is handy for finishing every bit of this delicious sauce.

SALAD CONDE DE ORGAZ

1 head Bibb lettuce, cored,
   washed, and quartered
4 strips pimiento

4 hearts of palm, halved
2 artichoke hearts, halved
   VINAIGRETTE DRESSING

Line 4 chilled salad plates with the lettuce. Wrap a pimiento strip around the base of each split heart of palm and place in the center of the lettuce. Lay half an artichoke heart beside. Drizzle with dressing and serve.

VINAIGRETTE DRESSING

½ cup olive oil
   Juice of 2 lemons
1 egg yolk
2 teaspoons red wine vinegar
½ teaspoon water
¼ teaspoon sugar

Salt and freshly ground
   black pepper
½ teaspoon Dijon mustard
½ teaspoon Worcestershire
   sauce

1. Mix the oil and lemon juice. Beat into the egg yolk.
2. Add the vinegar and water, beating well.
3. Add the remaining ingredients, combining thoroughly. Refrigerate before using.

FILET OF SOLE SABBAGH

2 pounds filet of sole
2 cups dry white wine
¼ cup butter

4 bananas, cut in strips
   HOLLANDAISE SAUCE

1. Place the fish in a poaching pan. Add the wine, bring to a simmer, and poach gently for 8 to 10 minutes. Drain.
2. Melt the butter over medium heat. Add the sliced bananas and sauté just to heat through.
3. Place the fish on a heat-proof platter. Arrange the bananas evenly over. Cover with Hollandaise Sauce. Brown lightly under a hot broiler.

HOLLANDAISE SAUCE

3 egg yolks
½ teaspoon salt
¼ teaspoon white pepper

1 tablespoon lemon juice
¼ pound plus 1 tablespoon
   butter, melted

1. Place the egg yolks, salt, pepper, and lemon juice in the top of a double boiler over hot—not boiling—water.
2. Beat until the mixture begins to thicken, 5 to 15 minutes.
3. Add the butter one tablespoon at a time, beating constantly. If the butter is added too rapidly, the sauce will break. Remove from heat.

Hollandaise sauce may be held for a short time over warm water in a double boiler.

FLÁN

1 cup sugar
2 cups milk
  Zest of ½ orange

Zest of ½ lemon
½ stick cinnamon
4 eggs

1. Preheat oven to 325°.
2. Place ½ cup sugar in a small pan and heat slowly until melted and golden. Pour into 4 individual custard cups, turning to coat the sides and bottoms evenly.
3. Bring the milk, both zests, and cinnamon to a boil. Remove from heat and allow to cool slightly.
4. Beat the eggs with the remaining ½ cup sugar. Stir in a little of the cooled milk, then add the remainder of the milk and beat to combine. Pour into the caramel-lined custard cups.
5. Place the cups in a deep baking pan. Add cold water to half the depth of the cups. Bake in preheated oven 1 hour or until set.
6. Refrigerate until ready to serve. Turn out on dessert plates.

This is a light custard that, when turned out of the mold, appears to have had caramel poured over it.

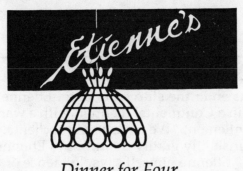

Dinner for Four

Soupe aux Cerises

Moules Ravigote

Rognons de Veau Flambés

Endives Meunière

Bananes Flambées aux Amandes

Wines:

With the Mussels—Vouvray

With the Kidneys—Pomerol

With the Bananes—Veuve-Clicquot Brut Champagne

Myrl and Etienne Gluck, Owners

Roger Lenoir, Executive Chef

Gerald Aimee, Head Chef

As patrons enter the stucco building, Etienne Gluck greets the ladies in a Continental manner, with a warm handshake for the gentlemen. "We have a critical clientele that we cater to and we want to instantly gratify them," says Etienne's wife Myrl. "It takes teamwork," Etienne himself says. Evidence of the level of teamwork at Etienne's may be found in the longevity of the employees. Chef Roger Lenoir has been running the kitchen for twenty-eight years. As for the rest of the staff, one waiter puts it succinctly: "There's no such thing as a job opening up at Etienne's. You could wait for years."

The setting is elegant, tastefully done in deep blue and white, with gleaming gold-and-crystal chandeliers and Tiffany-style hanging lamps. Porcelains are trimmed in blue and gold with "Etienne" in gold inscription. Room dividers create a sense of intimacy in the upper-level dining area; downstairs is the bar and entertainment lounge with its etched and airbrushed thirty-two-foot mirror by David Stevens.

Chef Lenoir is well known for his creative cooking, utilizing the best foods available and cooking them to perfection. "We are proud of the food we serve," says Mrs. Gluck. The cuisine is "wholesome French food, the portions being generous. We don't make toy food." Popular items include frogs' legs, Dover sole, steaks, and several duck and veal dishes.

Twenty years ago Etienne's took Horace Greeley's proverbial advice and moved to downtown Phoenix from Cleveland; sixteen years later, a growing reputation and clientele made it desirable to relocate to La Posada resort in Scottsdale when the opportunity arose. There is now a second Etienne's, with the same menu and decor, in Palm Desert, California.

La Posada Resort
4949 East Lincoln Drive
Scottsdale

SOUPE AUX CERISES
Cherry Soup

¼ pound butter
1½ tablespoons flour
3 cups pitted fresh cherries
¾ cup sugar (approximately)

3 to 4 tablespoons kirsch
4 slices thin French bread
(baguette)

1. Melt 1½ tablespoons butter in a saucepan over medium heat. Add the flour and cook, stirring constantly, for 5 minutes.
2. Gradually stir in 1½ quarts warm water. Add the cherries and up to ¾ cup sugar, depending on the tartness of the cherries. Add the kirsch.
3. Bring the soup to a boil and cook until the cherries are very tender.
4. Melt the remaining butter over medium heat. Add the bread and sauté on all sides until golden. Place in a soup tureen.
5. Pour the soup over and serve immediately.

MOULES RAVIGOTE
Mussels Ravigote

2 quarts mussels
BOUQUET GARNI
(see next page)
4 black peppercorns
1 medium-size onion, sliced
½ cup dry white wine
1½ tablespoons white wine
vinegar

¼ cup oil
1½ teaspoons capers
1 teaspoon chopped parsley
1 teaspoon chives
1 teaspoon tarragon
1 teaspoon freshly ground
black pepper

1. Scrub and rinse the mussels. Place in a kettle with the Bouquet Garni, peppercorns, onion, and wine. Steam until opened; discard any that do not open.
2. Remove the mussels and discard the shells. Set the meats aside.
3. Strain the pot liquid through several layers of cheesecloth. Return to heat and simmer until reduced by half. Allow to cool.
4. Combine the remaining ingredients. Add ½ cup of the reduced pot liquid. Taste for seasonings and adjust as needed.
5. Add the mussels. Refrigerate before serving.

These may be served in a goodly amount of their sauce, or hors d'oeuvre-style on toothpicks or toast circlets.

BOUQUET GARNI

1 bay leaf
2 sprigs fresh thyme

4 sprigs fresh parsley

Tie with thread in a small bundle.

ROGNONS DE VEAU FLAMBÉS
Flambéed Veal Kidneys

4 small veal kidneys,
   cleaned and skinned
4 tablespoons butter
4 large mushrooms, sliced
2 tablespoons brandy,
   warmed

Salt and pepper to taste
⅛ teaspoon dry mustard
2 tablespoons whipping
   cream

1. Sauté the kidneys in the butter over high heat until almost done. Remove from the pan and set aside.
2. In the same butter, sauté the mushrooms until tender. Remove and set aside.
3. Cook the pan juices to reduce to about 2 tablespoons. Slice the kidneys crosswise about ½" thick. Return to the pan; add the brandy and flame.
4. Add the mushrooms, salt, pepper, and dry mustard. Stir well.
5. Remove the kidneys and mushrooms to a heated serving platter. Stir the cream into the pan juices. Heat, but do not allow to boil. Pour the sauce over the kidneys and serve.

ENDIVES MEUNIÈRE

12 Belgian endives
6 tablespoons butter

Juice of 1 lemon
Salt

1. Trim, wash, and dry the endives. Melt the butter in a heavy pan over low heat. Add the endives and cook, turning occasionally, for 30 to 40 minutes or until golden brown on all sides and very tender.
2. Remove to a hot serving dish. Sprinkle with lemon juice and lightly season with salt to taste. Pour the browned butter over and serve very hot.

BANANES FLAMBÉES AUX AMANDES

6 ripe bananas, peeled and halved crosswise
Juice of ½ lemon
1 teaspoon butter, melted
3 tablespoons sugar

⅓ cup blanched slivered almonds
¼ cup brandy or Curaçao, warmed

1. Preheat oven to 400°.
2. Arrange the bananas close together in a shallow baking dish. Add ¼ cup water and sprinkle with the lemon juice, melted butter, sugar, and slivered almonds. Bake in preheated oven, basting occasionally and adding a little more water if necessary, for 20 minutes or until soft and beginning to glaze.
3. Bring the bananas and the warmed spirits to the table. Flame the spirits with a match and pour over the bananas. Shake the dish gently until the flame dies and serve.

The bananas may be baked ahead of time and reheated in a chafing dish at the table if desired.

Dinner for Six

Herbed Liver Pâté Maison

Cold Hungarian Black Cherry Soup

English Spinach Salad with Light Mustard Dressing

Stuffed Trout del Mar

Vegetable Sauté au Fines Herbes

Fresh Strawberry Rum Tart

Wine:

Chateau Montelena Chardonnay

Lee and Harriet Finch, Owners

FINCH'S

Finch's is tucked away behind the old Windmill Dinner Theater in Scottsdale. A small, intimate restaurant complete with candlelight and fresh flowers on each table, Finch's offers patrons a comfortable European dining experience. "The food and European-style black-tie service are what Finch's is all about," says chef-owner Lee Finch. The limited, *prix-fixée* menu includes various classical standards as well as unique originals; in addition, Chef Finch nightly creates a dinner special which takes advantage of market offerings.

The complete dinners include a pâté maison with cucumber dills and French bread, a hot or cold soup, a salad with familiar or exotic dressings, and sautéed fresh vegetables in season. Desserts include such specialties as rum custard ice cream topped with coconut rum liqueur and shredded coconut, amaretto-flavored cheesecake, or Swiss chocolate almond mousse. Finch's has been famous since its inception for its Beef Wellington and Roast Duck Rockefeller. An extensive wine list, covering all price ranges, and a large selection of after-dinner liqueurs are also available to complement the menu.

10305 North Scottsdale Road
Scottsdale

HERBED LIVER PÂTÉ MAISON

1 cup chopped onions
¼ pound plus 4 tablespoons
   butter
1 teaspoon salt
½ teaspoon pepper

½ teaspoon ground thyme
½ teaspoon ground oregano
1 bay leaf
1 pound chicken livers
2 to 3 tablespoons brandy

1. In a skillet, sauté the onions with the butter, salt, pepper, thyme, oregano, and bay leaf until the onions are lightly browned.
2. Add the chicken livers and continue cooking just until the livers are no longer pink inside.
3. Place in a blender with the brandy and process until smooth. (If using a food processor, refrigerate the liver mixture until firm before processing.) Remove to a mold and refrigerate until set.

Serve with sliced French bread and thinly sliced dill pickles.

COLD HUNGARIAN BLACK CHERRY SOUP

1 (16-ounce) can pitted
   sweet black cherries
1 cup cherry juice
¼ cup sugar
2 teaspoons cornstarch
¼ teaspoon salt

¼ teaspoon cinnamon
1 cup burgundy
3 drops almond extract
   (optional)
Brandy to taste (optional)
6 tablespoons sour cream

Chop the cherries medium-finely. Place in a 2-quart saucepan with the cherry juice, sugar, cornstarch, salt, and cinnamon. Simmer, stirring constantly, until thickened. Remove from heat and add the wine, almond extract, and brandy, if desired. Chill at least 3 hours. Top each serving with 1 tablespoon sour cream.

ENGLISH SPINACH SALAD
with Light Mustard Dressing

2 to 3 *bunches spinach*
1 *apple*
½ *cup sliced toasted almonds*
½ *cup chopped green onions*

6 *strips bacon, cooked*
  and crumbled
LIGHT MUSTARD
DRESSING

1. Thoroughly wash the spinach, discarding any leathery leaves and tough stems. Drain well or spin dry and place on a large chilled salad plate.
2. Core and dice the apple. Arrange over the spinach with the almonds, green onions, and bacon bits. Drizzle with dressing to taste and serve.

LIGHT MUSTARD DRESSING

1 *cup salad oil*
¼ *cup olive oil*
1 *teaspoon salt*
2 *teaspoons sugar*
1½ *tablespoons Colman's dry*
  mustard

6 *tablespoons tarragon wine*
  vinegar
2 *tablespoons water*
⅛ *teaspoon white pepper*

Thoroughly combine the ingredients by whisking or shaking. Chill; recombine before use.

STUFFED TROUT DEL MAR

¼ pound fresh mushrooms, sliced
½ cup white wine
1 teaspoon Worcestershire sauce
1 teaspoon finely diced shallots
3 to 4 drops Tabasco sauce
½ teaspoon salt
¼ teaspoon pepper
Zest of ½ orange, finely grated
Zest of ½ lemon, finely grated
1 tablespoon orange juice
1 tablespoon lemon juice

¼ cup chopped fresh parsley
¼ cup sliced raw scallops
½ teaspoon whole thyme
½ teaspoon rosemary
⅛ teaspoon garlic powder
¼ cup king or snow crabmeat
¼ cup bay shrimp
2½ cups coarse French bread crumbs
¼ pound butter, melted
6 (8 to 10-ounce) trout, cleaned
SHERRY-LEMON BUTTER (see next page)
Lemon wedges or slices
Parsley or watercress sprigs

1. Place the mushrooms, wine, Worcestershire sauce, shallots, Tabasco sauce, salt, and pepper in a saucepan. Bring to a boil. Cook until the liquid has evaporated.

2. Add the orange and lemon zest, fruit juices, parsley, scallops, thyme, rosemary, and garlic powder. Simmer until the liquid has almost evaporated. Remove from heat.

3. Add the crabmeat, shrimp, bread crumbs, and butter; mix thoroughly. Taste for seasoning and adjust if necessary. Allow the mixture to cool.

4. Preheat oven to 400°. Generously stuff the trout with the filling. Cover the bottom of a baking dish with the Sherry-Lemon Butter. Lay the trout over and bake 35 to 45 minutes or until the fish flakes easily.

5. Garnish with lemon wedges or slices and sprigs of greenery. Serve immediately.

SHERRY-LEMON BUTTER

¼ pound butter, melted
2 tablespoons sherry
1 teaspoon lemon juice

2 drops Tabasco sauce
Salt and pepper to taste

Combine all ingredients.

VEGETABLE SAUTÉ AU FINES HERBES

1 zucchini
1 yellow squash
1 summer squash
1 tablespoon salt

¼ pound mushrooms, sliced
1 tablespoon Spice Islands
   Fines Herbes
¼ pound butter

1. Wash the zucchini, yellow squash, and summer squash and slice ¼" thick.
2. Bring 3 quarts of water and the salt to a boil. Blanch the vegetables for about 1½ minutes or until fork-tender. Drain and cool.
3. Sauté the mushrooms and fines herbes in the butter until golden. Add the blanched vegetables and sauté to heat through. Serve immediately.

FRESH STRAWBERRY RUM TART

1 egg
1 egg yolk
3 tablespoons sugar
3 tablespoons flour
2 teaspoons unflavored
   gelatin
¾ cup milk, hot
2 egg whites, stiffly beaten
½ cup whipping cream,
   whipped

2 tablespoons Jamaican rum
6 pre-baked pastry tart shells
2 cups fresh strawberries,
   washed and hulled
3 tablespoons red currant
   jelly
1 tablespoon brandy
½ cup chopped pistachio nuts

1. In a saucepan, beat the whole egg, egg yolk, sugar, and flour until the mixture is light and fluffy.
2. Soften the gelatin in 1 tablespoon cold water, then dissolve in the milk. Add to the egg mixture.
3. Cook over moderate heat, stirring constantly, until hot and thick. Do not allow to boil. Allow to cool.
4. Fold in the beaten egg whites, whipped cream, and rum. Spoon into the baked tart shells. Arrange the strawberries over.
5. Melt the currant jelly and thin with the brandy. Drizzle over the strawberries. Sprinkle with chopped pistachios.

To cool the thickened egg mixture rapidly, set the saucepan into a bowl filled with cracked ice and stir.

Garcia's las Villas

Dinner for Six

Ensalada Mexicana

Pollo Fundido

Spanish Rice

Mango Delight

Beverages:

Before dinner—Margaritas

With the meal—Margaritas or beer

Garcia's of Scottsdale, Owners

GARCIA'S

Garcia's Las Villas traces its roots back to the 1950s, when Julio and Olivia Garcia opened a small take-out restaurant in Phoenix. As it flourished, it was changed over to a regular dinner establishment. In the late sixties a second location was opened in Scottsdale, and a third in northwest Phoenix in 1978. Finally, Garcia's Las Villas was opened in 1980 to crown the Garcia's success.

The building was designed by architect David Stevens. It was inspired by an impressive restaurant in Mexico City, from which it draws its massive semicircular stained-glass windows and cathedral columns. Bold colors are utilized in this three-tiered dining environment. The lowest level is graced with a skylight, providing natural lighting for the array of plants hanging from the high ceilings. The upper tiers provide more intimate private dining for those who prefer it.

"Our restaurants are informal and very Phoenician," says Mr. Garcia. "We want our guests to feel at home and to relax." The bright colors, large Mexican-style flower arrangements, and piñatas dangling from the ceilings help to provide a festive atmosphere. A cozy cocktail lounge with a view of the village tennis club also helps take the edge off a tough day or makes the wait for a table a pleasure.

4420 East Camelback Road
Phoenix

GARCIA'S

ENSALADA MEXICANA

1 *head iceberg lettuce*
¼ *head romaine lettuce*
¼ *head purple cabbage, sliced*
2 *carrots, shaved*
1 *cup salad dressing*
2 *avocados*

2 *tomatoes, diced*
1 *cup grated longhorn cheese*
¼ *cup grated Jack cheese*
¼ *cup finely chopped green onions*
½ *cup olives*

1. Wash and dry the lettuces. Tear into bite-size pieces. Toss with the cabbage and carrots and distribute on 4 salad plates. Sprinkle each with ¼ cup dressing.
2. Remove the pits and skins from the avocados. Slice each into 8 pieces.
3. Arrange over the salads, in order, the tomatoes, longhorn cheese, Jack cheese, green onions, and olives. Top each with 4 slices avocado.

A blue cheese, Thousand Island, or vinaigrette dressing is recommended.

POLLO FUNDIDO

1 large or 2 small chickens
1 clove garlic, mashed
2 tablespoons salt
3 stalks celery
1 bell pepper
  VEGETABLE GESADO
  (see next page)
8 (12") flour tortillas
1 cup oil for frying
1 pound cream cheese,
  room temperature

½ pint whipping cream
2 cups shredded longhorn
  cheese
½ head purple cabbage
2 tablespoons chopped
  green onion
1 tomato, sliced
6 olives

1. Place the whole chickens, garlic, salt, celery, and the seeds and pulp from the center of the bell pepper in a 4-quart pot. (Reserve pepper for Vegetable Gesado.) Add 2 quarts water. Bring to a boil, reduce heat, cover, and cook about 1 hour or until tender, skimming periodically to remove the foam that rises to the surface.

2. Remove the chickens and allow to cool. Strain the stock, return to heat in a clean pot, and cook until reduced by half. Degrease by laying strips of paper toweling across the surface to absorb the fat. Reserve stock for Vegetable Gesado.

3. Bone the chickens. Mix with the Vegetable Gesado.

4. Preheat oven to 350°.

5. Spread about ½ cup chicken mixture down the center of each tortilla. Fold about 2" of each end of the tortilla over. Fold one side of the tortilla over and roll up the stuffed tortilla in a neat package. Fasten with wooden toothpicks, making sure the ends are sealed.

6. Heat the oil over medium heat. Fry the stuffed tortillas, turning to brown evenly, for 2 to 3 minutes or until golden. Drain on paper toweling.

7. Whip the cream cheese until fluffy, then whip in the cream. Cut each tortilla roll into 3 pieces and place on a baking sheet. Top each piece with about 1 tablespoon cream cheese mixture. Sprinkle with grated longhorn cheese.

8. Bake in preheated oven for 10 minutes. Arrange on leaves of purple cabbage, sprinkle with green onion, place tomato slices on the side, and garnish with olives on toothpicks.

GARCIA'S

VEGETABLE GESADO

5 tablespoons oil	1 clove garlic, minced
3 stalks celery, finely chopped	1½ teaspoons salt
	1 teaspoon pepper
1 bell pepper (from Pollo Fundido preparation), finely chopped	2 cups chicken stock (from Pollo Fundido preparation)
1 white onion, finely chopped	
½ pound canned whole tomatoes	

Heat the oil in a frying pan to 300° over medium heat. Add the celery, bell pepper, and onion and sauté until tender. Crush the tomatoes and add with their juice. Add the garlic, salt, pepper, and chicken stock. Simmer 30 minutes. Allow to cool before using.

SPANISH RICE

1½ cups long-grain rice	¼ cup chicken base
¼ cup salad oil	¼ cup tomato purée
1 clove garlic, minced	¼ cup mashed peeled tomato
½ cup chopped white onion	½ teaspoon pepper

1. Place the rice, oil, garlic, and onion in a saucepan over low heat. Brown lightly, stirring occasionally. Pour off excess oil, leaving about 1 tablespoon.
2. Stir in the chicken base, tomato purée, mashed tomato, and pepper. Add 1 quart cold water. Bring to a boil, reduce heat, cover, and simmer 30 minutes or until the liquid is absorbed.

MANGO DELIGHT

1 (16-ounce) can sliced mangos	½ cup Cool-Whip
	Whipped cream or Cool-Whip for garnish
1 pint fresh strawberries, hulled	

Drain the mangos and cut each slice in half. Slice 4 strawberries and reserve; combine the remainder with the mangos and ½ cup Cool-Whip. Spoon into dessert cups. Top with whipped cream or more Cool-Whip and garnish with the sliced strawberries.

GREAT AMERICAN SEAFOOD CO. Est. 1977

Dinner for Six

Clams Casino

Vichyssoise

Baked Lobster

Broccoli with Hollandaise

Apple Crisp

Admiral's Coffee

Wine:

Château St. Jean Chardonnay

Richard McClellan, Owner

Terry Dirodis, Manager

GREAT AMERICAN SEAFOOD COMPANY

"**We** opened the Great American Seafood Company because fresh seafood was very limited in Phoenix," says owner Dick McClellan. "We offer the freshest seafood available; our menu necessarily changes with the seasons. When king salmon or soft-shell crabs are available, they are on our menu. Our market-board menus reflect the flexibility of buying only what is available fresh on any given day in the market."

The cuisine ranges from classical American to Continental gourmet. Fish broiled over mesquite charcoal is a specialty of the house, whether it be salmon, swordfish, haddock, or other fresh fish as available. More elaborate preparations include Truite en Croûte, Lobster Cardinal, and Pompano en Papillote. For dry-landers, prime rib of beef and mesquite-broiled barbecued chicken are also available. All the recipes were developed by the McClellan family. "Our most popular dessert—the Apple Crisp—is from an old family recipe," says Dick.

The restaurant's lobby is done in native Arizona stone, with a built-in lobster tank. Behind the captain's station—which came off an Australian ship—a chalkboard announces the fresh seafood arrivals. Passing the all-brass binnacle, one enters a Cape Cod setting complete with plank floors, paneled walls, and tables set with brass replica whale-oil lamps. A local artist has done seafood collages which join a marlin and a sailfish on the walls. One of the three dining areas has a wood-burning fireplace in frequent use.

4900 East Indian School Road
Phoenix

CLAMS CASINO

4 tablespoons butter	1 cup bread crumbs
½ cup minced onion greens or chives	2 tablespoons minced bell pepper
½ teaspoon freshly ground black pepper	2 tablespoons minced fresh parsley
½ teaspoon thyme	2 dozen cherrystone clams, on the half shell
2 tablespoons fresh lemon juice	3 slices bacon, diced

1. Preheat oven to 400°.
2. Melt the butter. Combine with the remaining ingredients except the clams and bacon.
3. Top each clam with a spoonful of the mixture. Garnish with the bacon. Bake in preheated oven for 15 minutes or until the bacon is crisp.

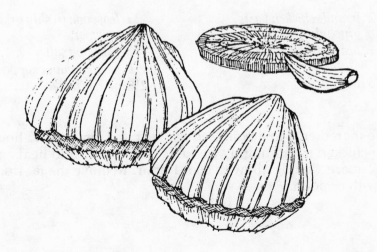

VICHYSSOISE

¼ pound butter
3 cups sliced leeks
½ cup chopped celery
2 quarts CHICKEN STOCK
4 cups sliced potatoes

2 cups whipping cream
Salt
White pepper
¼ cup finely chopped chives

1. Melt the butter. Add the leeks and celery; sauté until translucent.
2. Add the Chicken Stock and potatoes. Simmer until the potatoes are cooked through.
3. Transfer to a blender or food processor and purée. Allow to cool and place in the refrigerator until chilled.
4. Before serving, stir in the cream. Season to taste with salt and white pepper. Garnish each serving with the chopped chives.

Onions may be substituted for the leeks in a pinch.

CHICKEN STOCK

2 pounds chicken parts,
   including skin
1 heart of celery, including
   leaves, chopped
3 bay leaves

¼ teaspoon freshly ground
   pepper
½ teaspoon salt
1 small onion, chopped
2½ quarts water

Bring the ingredients to a boil. Reduce heat and simmer 1½ hours or until the chicken is thoroughly cooked. Strain; return to heat and reduce to 2 quarts liquid. Allow to cool 1 hour. Remove the fat from the surface with a spoon.

BAKED LOBSTER

6 (1-pound) live Maine
  lobsters
1 pound mushrooms, chopped
¼ pound butter
2 cups BÉCHAMEL SAUCE
1 pound shrimp, cooked
  and shelled

1 cup whipping cream
4 egg yolks
2 tablespoons brandy
Salt and pepper to taste
Parmesan cheese

1. Cook the lobsters in boiling water for 12 to 15 minutes, or until the shells are bright orange-red and the tails are tightly curled.
2. Remove the legs and claws. With a heavy, serrated knife, cut through each shell down the back from the base of the head to the tail. Remove the meat from the body and claws, reserving the shells.
3. Sauté the lobster meat and mushrooms in the butter over medium-high heat until the mushrooms are tender. Add to the Béchamel Sauce.
4. Add the shrimp, cream, and egg yolks to the mixture. Stir in the brandy, salt, and pepper.
5. Refill the lobster shells with the mixture. Place on a baking sheet and sprinkle with Parmesan cheese. Broil 5 minutes or until lightly browned.

BÉCHAMEL SAUCE

4 tablespoons butter
6 tablespoons flour
½ cup Fish Stock (see index)

½ cup milk
Salt and pepper to taste
⅛ teaspoon nutmeg

1. Melt the butter in a saucepan. Add the flour and cook, whisking constantly, for 4 to 5 minutes. Do not allow to brown.
2. Stir in the remaining ingredients. Simmer until thick and bubbly, stirring constantly.

BROCCOLI WITH HOLLANDAISE

1 *large bunch fresh broccoli*
8 *egg yolks, room temperature*
1 *tablespoon lemon juice*
¼ *cup dry white wine*

½ *teaspoon salt*
Dash of cayenne pepper
½ *pound butter, clarified*

1. Trim the thick stems off the broccoli. Cut into 6 portions. Steam 15 minutes or until tender.
2. Place the egg yolks, lemon juice, wine, salt, and cayenne in a stainless-steel bowl over simmering water. Whisk vigorously until soft peaks form, about 5 minutes. Remove from heat and slowly add the butter in a thin stream, beating constantly.
3. Place the broccoli on a serving platter or individual plates. Cover with Hollandaise sauce and serve.

Note: If the sauce separates, immediately whisk in 1 to 2 tablespoons boiling water to restore it.

The better the wine, the better the Hollandaise will be.

APPLE CRISP

12 *apples*	1 *teaspoon salt*
2 *tablespoons lemon juice*	¾ *teaspoon cinnamon*
½ *pound butter, softened*	*Whipped cream*
2 *cups brown sugar*	
2 *cups flour*	

1. Preheat oven to 350°.
2. Peel and slice the apples. Arrange in a baking pan. Sprinkle with the lemon juice.
3. Cream the butter and sugar together. Mix in the flour, salt, and cinnamon. Sprinkle over the apples.
4. Bake in preheated oven for 20 to 30 minutes or until golden brown. Serve with a generous garnish of whipped cream.

ADMIRAL'S COFFEE

6 *cups freshly brewed coffee*	4½ *ounces crème de menthe*
9 *ounces brown crème* *de cacao*	*Whipped cream*

To each cup of fresh hot coffee, add a jigger of crème de cacao and ½ jigger of crème de menthe. Top with whipped cream.

the Impeccable Pig

Dinner for Six

Cream of Asparagus Soup

Tossed Salad with Mustard-Herb Dressing

Chicken Scallops Sauté Meunière

Long-Grain and Wild Rice

Parker House Rolls

Kiwi Sherbet

Wines:

With the dinner—St. Clement Sauvignon Blanc, 1980,
or
Joseph Phelps Chardonnay, 1979

With the Sherbet—Mosel Auslese, J.J. Prüm, 1979

Dee Ann Skipton, Owner

On the sidewalk are French flower carts, antique park benches, and an assortment of decorative items. Inside, owner Dee Ann Skipton has decorated with a flair for the unusual—quilts, baskets, copper, antique furniture, even animals from antique carousels. It may not seem like an ordinary restaurant—it isn't. Dee Ann always felt that a combination of an antique shop and a restaurant would prove popular, and she was right. "World travelers come by and exclaim, 'This is wonderful! I've never seen anything like it,' " she says.

The main dining area is elevated, providing patrons with a view of the open kitchen as well as glimpses of the three other rooms. The Garden, just inside the entrance, is lush with greenery and a fountain. The Red Room tends to have the more elegant antiques, while the Barn lures those interested in primitive, folk, and American art. Guests dine on antique furniture, both in the main area and among the antique settings, which change from day to day as items are sold and replaced.

"I truly feel that the public becomes my guest when they enter the Impeccable Pig," says Dee Ann. "I want them to enjoy their experience here and to look forward to returning. Our food is prepared fresh and with special care; the portions are generous and all meals are served with our homemade rolls, prepared on the premises daily." Entrées are posted on a chalkboard and change daily. There are also a selection of desserts ranging from fresh Missouri berries to rum cake, and a wine list with a well-chosen variety.

7042 East Indian School Road
Scottsdale

CREAM OF ASPARAGUS SOUP

1 tablespoon butter	Salt and pepper to taste
1 small onion, finely chopped	¼ teaspoon mace
½ stalk celery, finely chopped	¾ cup whipping cream
2 cups Chicken Stock (see index)	3 hard-cooked eggs, chopped
1 pound asparagus tips, chopped	

1. Melt the butter in a saucepan over medium heat. Add the onion and celery and cook, stirring often, until soft but not brown.
2. Add the stock and bring to a boil. Add the asparagus; simmer for 5 minutes.
3. Add the salt, pepper, and mace. Remove from heat. Slowly stir in the cream.
4. Reheat gently. Serve in bowls garnished with hard-cooked egg.

TOSSED SALAD WITH MUSTARD-HERB DRESSING

1 bunch broccoli
1 bunch watercress
1 head Boston leaf lettuce
1 head iceberg lettuce
2 tomatoes, cut into wedges

12 mushrooms, cleaned and sliced
MUSTARD-HERB DRESSING

1. Cut the broccoli into florets. Steam 5 minutes; drain.
2. Core and wash the watercress and lettuces. Shake off excess moisture and tear into bite-size pieces. Place in individual salad bowls.
3. Arrange the broccoli, tomatoes, and mushrooms over. Toss with the dressing.

MUSTARD-HERB DRESSING

1 clove garlic
2 green onions, minced
½ teaspoon Dijon mustard
2 teaspoons salt
½ teaspoon freshly ground black pepper

1 teaspoon sugar
⅓ cup red wine vinegar
1 tablespoon dried basil
1 tablespoon dried tarragon
1 teaspoon celery seed
1 cup cottonseed oil

Place all ingredients except the oil in a blender. Process until well blended. With the machine still on, add the oil in a slow, steady stream.

CHICKEN SCALLOPS SAUTÉ MEUNIÈRE

12 single chicken breasts,
   boned and skinned
Salt
Pepper
Flour for dredging

3 eggs, beaten
½ pound butter
Juice of 2 lemons
Chopped fresh parsley

1. Place the chicken breasts one at a time on a large sheet of waxed paper. Sprinkle with a few drops of water and cover with another sheet of waxed paper. Pound flat with a meat mallet or the flat of a cleaver. Cut into medallions.

2. Sprinkle the chicken with salt and pepper. Dredge in flour and dip in the beaten eggs. Melt a little of the butter in a pan over medium-high heat and sauté the chicken until golden brown on both sides, adding more butter as needed. Remove the chicken to a heated platter, reserving the pan butter.

3. Add the lemon juice to the butter in the pan. Whisk over low heat until reduced to a thin sauce consistency. Pour over the chicken. Garnish with chopped parsley.

LONG-GRAIN AND WILD RICE

¼ *pound butter*
1½ *cups long-grain rice*
½ *cup wild rice*

1 *cup chopped onions*
1 *quart Chicken Stock (see index) or bouillon*

1. Melt the butter in a saucepan with a tight-fitting lid. Pour off half and reserve. To the remainder, add both rices and the onions. Shake the pan until all the grains are coated with butter.
2. Add the stock. Bring to a simmer and cook 20 to 25 minutes or until all the stock is absorbed.
3. Add the reserved melted butter and toss with a fork.

PARKER HOUSE ROLLS

1 *package active dry yeast*
1 *cup warm water (114°)*
½ *cup sugar*
½ *teaspoon salt*

1 *egg, beaten*
½ *cup Crisco shortening*
3 *cups all-purpose flour*
2 *tablespoons butter, melted*

1. Dissolve the yeast in the warm water. Stir in the sugar, salt, and beaten egg.
2. Place the shortening in a bread bowl. Pour the yeast mixture over and mix with a spoon. Gradually add the flour, 1 cup at a time, and mix until a somewhat sticky dough is formed.
3. Turn out onto a floured surface. Roll out to ¼" thickness. Cut with a biscuit cutter.
4. Place on a baking sheet. Pat with the melted butter and fold in half. Pinch closed. Let rise until doubled in bulk, about 1 hour.
5. Bake the rolls at 350° for 15 minutes.

KIWI SHERBET

1 *package unflavored gelatin*
2 *eggs, separated*
1 *cup sugar*
¼ *teaspoon salt*
2 *teaspoons Grand Marnier liqueur*

2 *cups peeled, crushed kiwi fruit (approximately)*
Sliced fresh kiwi fruit (optional)

1. Soak the gelatin in ¼ cup cold water for 5 minutes. Place in the top of a double boiler over boiling water and stir until dissolved.

2. Beat the egg yolks well, then beat in ¾ cup sugar, the salt, Grand Marnier, and crushed kiwi fruit. When well mixed, beat in the dissolved gelatin. Mix thoroughly and freeze in ice cube trays.

3. When frozen, place in a chilled bowl and break into chunks. Beat with an electric mixer until smooth and fluffy.

4. Beat the egg whites until soft peaks form. Gradually add the remaining ¼ cup sugar and beat until stiff. Fold into the kiwi mixture. Place in a covered container and return to the freezer until firm, stirring occasionally. Serve garnished with sliced kiwi if desired.

ORE HOUSE.

Dinner for Four

Stuffed Mushrooms

Combination Lahvosh

Filet Ore House

Mud Pie

Wines:

Chappellet Cabernet Sauvignon, 1976

Beaujolais-Villages, Jaboulet-Vercherre, 1978

John Beaupre and Scott Hopman, Owners

Rick Swartz, Manager

JOHN SCOTT'S ORE HOUSE

John Scott's Ore House derives its name from owners John Beaupre and Scott Hopman, who opened the first Ore House in the Idaho mining region of Sun Valley. The Ore House is known for good, hearty food at reasonable prices and for its casual, convivial atmosphere. At first, the Ore House reputation relied on steak and a flair for providing a good time. More recently, however, the Ore House has responded to the change in American dining preferences by adding seafood, salads in abundance, and specialty items to the menu. In fact, such marine entrées as Smoked Alaskan Cod, Salmon Filet, and a fresh catch of the day now outnumber the steaks on the menu at the Phoenix Ore House.

The restaurant was designed to encourage a festive atmosphere with the option of more intimate dining. The second-level dining room overlooks the downstairs bar, allowing patrons to watch the action below or to converse quietly among themselves; also, patio dining is available in the milder months. In the bar, a skylight set in the high ceiling provides light for the numerous plants suspended there. A Southwestern theme warms the whole place with its stucco arches, Indian art, and blue and earth-tone decor.

Manager Rick Swartz sees his task as being to provide a good meal with the opportunity of participating in some fun. The staff is encouraged toward the casual and friendly rather than the formal. Ticket stubs from many of the area's sporting events and ski lifts are accepted as two-for-one coupons for drinks in the bar after six o'clock during the week; disco music gets the place hopping after the dinner hour. "We want our guests to leave with the feeling that they had some fun and an enjoyable experience, that the waiters and waitresses were pleasant, and that they were served well," Rick says.

5645 North 19th Avenue
Phoenix

STUFFED MUSHROOMS

1 *pound fresh mushrooms*
¼ *cup minced shallots*
½ *cup grated Parmesan
    cheese*

¼ *cup olive oil*

1. Preheat oven to 450°.
2. Remove the mushroom stems from the caps. Chop the stems and mix with the shallots and cheese. Fill the caps with the mixture, rounding well.
3. Sprinkle each mushroom with 2 to 3 drops of olive oil. Dip the bottom of each cap in oil and place on a baking sheet. Bake in preheated oven for 8 minutes.

COMBINATION LAHVOSH

⅓ *cup sliced mushrooms*
1 *large (pizza-size) lahvosh
    cracker, broken into
    small pieces*
3 *ounces king crabmeat*

½ *tomato, peeled, seeded,
    and coarsely chopped*
¼ *cup chopped Canadian
    bacon*
¼ *pound Dofino cheese, sliced*

1. Preheat oven to 450°.
2. Sauté the mushrooms in butter until very tender. Remove from heat and drain.
3. Place the crackers on a baking sheet. Cover with separate layers of crabmeat, chopped tomatoes, mushrooms, and Canadian bacon. Top each with sliced cheese.
4. Bake in preheated oven for 2 to 3 minutes or until the cheese is melted and bubbling.

FILET ORE HOUSE

4 (8-ounce) beef tenderloin
   filets
4 slices bacon
   ORE HOUSE MIXED
   VEGETABLES

¾ pound crabmeat
   BÉARNAISE SAUCE

Wrap the filets with bacon slices, using toothpicks to hold in place. Broil to desired doneness. Place on generous beds of mixed vegetables. Remove the toothpicks, top with crabmeat, and spoon Béarnaise Sauce over.

ORE HOUSE MIXED VEGETABLES

½ pound broccoli
½ pound cauliflower
¼ pound carrots

3 stalks celery
¼ pound zucchini

Trim the broccoli and cauliflower into florets. Slice the carrots, celery, and zucchini. Place the broccoli, cauliflower, carrots, and celery in a steamer over boiling water. Cover and cook 15 minutes. Add the zucchini and cook 10 minutes longer. Drain; keep warm.

BÉARNAISE SAUCE

2 tablespoons tarragon
   vinegar
½ teaspoon plus 1 pinch
   tarragon
¼ teaspoon chervil

¼ teaspoon minced scallion
2 peppercorns
6 egg yolks
½ pound butter, melted

1. Combine the vinegar, ½ teaspoon tarragon, chervil, scallion, and peppercorns in a small saucepan. Bring to a boil and cook until reduced by half. Strain and add the remaining pinch of tarragon. Keep warm.

(continued on next page)

2. Place the egg yolks in the top of a double boiler over barely simmering water. Whisk vigorously while adding the butter, tablespoon by tablespoon.

3. When all the butter has been incorporated, add the vinegar mixture in a slow, steady stream, whisking constantly. Continue whisking until a ribbon dropped from the whisk remains noticeable for 10 to 15 seconds. Remove from heat.

MUD PIE

2 dozen chocolate wafers	½ cup chocolate fudge, room temperature
¼ pound margarine, melted	
1 quart coffee ice cream	

1. With a rolling pin, crush the wafers into fine crumbs. Combine with the margarine and press into the bottom and sides of a 9" metal pie pan. Freeze 30 minutes.

2. Place the ice cream at room temperature to soften, about 20 minutes. Beat with an electric mixer until light and fluffy. Spread into the wafer crust and re-freeze for 1 hour.

3. Spread a thin layer of chocolate fudge over the ice cream. Keep in the freezer until ready to serve.

The trick to a light and fluffy mud pie is to whip the ice cream briskly to incorporate air into it.

MANDARIN DELIGHT

Dinner for Four

Pan-Fried Dumplings

Hot and Sour Soup

Lemon Chicken

Szechuan Shredded Beef with Hot Pepper Sauce

Eight-Treasure Chicken

Kung Pao Shrimp with Peanuts in Hot Sauce

Beverages:

With the Meal—Wan Fu wine or Tsing Tao beer

After Dinner—Tea

Charles Tsui, Owner

MANDARIN DELIGHT

Upon entering the Mandarin Delight, one is greeted by an Oriental statue overlooking a compelling red-and-black-checkerboard fountain. Folding screens serve as room dividers among the potted mums and greenery; Chinese lanterns hang from the ceiling, and the walls are flocked in red. The use of color in the decor, mostly red and black, is modest yet dramatic. A glass-enclosed gift case built at eye level into one wall holds ivory carvings, porcelain, and jewelry for patrons' inspection and, perhaps, purchase.

Owner Charles Tsui supervises all facets of the restaurant, as well as greeting guests and visiting tables to explain the menu. "I am proud of the food we serve," he says, "because every dish is prepared to keep the art of Chinese cooking at the highest standard. We prepare every dish from scratch when it is ordered. Because of our effort in the two years since we opened, Mandarin Delight has received numerous awards from various newspapers and magazines in the valley and is considered by many food critics to be the best Chinese restaurant. We take pride in serving our customers."

The house specialty is Peking Duck, which arrives tableside sizzling and crisp while the meat within is tender and moist. "The secret to Peking Duck is hanging the duck for eight hours prior to cooking. This allows the fats to drain and the skin to become very dry." The Mandarin Delight needs no advance notice to serve this specialty, since Mr. Tsui is able to estimate the number of requests for it nightly. Usually his estimates are prescient, though he admits that "upon occasion, my staff gets to eat a lot of Peking Duck." Other favorites include Lemon Chicken, Szechuan Shredded Beef, and Eight-Treasure Chicken, recipes for which Mr. Tsui is pleased to share with us.

5309 North 7th Street
Phoenix

MANDARIN DELIGHT

PAN-FRIED DUMPLINGS

⅔ pound Napa cabbage
⅔ pound ground pork
½ cup chopped green onions
2 tablespoons soy sauce
1 teaspoon salt
3 tablespoons sesame oil

¼ teaspoon black pepper
3 cups flour
¼ cup plus 1 tablespoon
 cooking oil
DIPPING SAUCE

1. Core the cabbage. Blanch in boiling water 2 minutes; squeeze dry and chop finely. Combine with the pork and green onions.
2. Mix together the soy sauce, salt, sesame oil, and black pepper. Add to the cabbage mixture and combine thoroughly. Set aside.
3. Place 2½ cups flour in a bowl. Add ⅔ cup boiling water a little at a time, stirring in with chopsticks. Add ⅓ cup cold water and combine. Dust a bread board with some of the remaining ½ cup flour; turn the dough out onto it. Flour your hands and knead until smooth, using more flour as necessary to prevent sticking. Let rest for 10 minutes.
4. Roll out as thin as possible in a 24" by 12" rectangle. Cut into 36 (4" by 2") sections.
5. Divide the reserved cabbage and pork mixture into 36 portions. Place one portion on each section of dough; fold in half and pinch the edges to seal.
6. Heat ¼ cup oil in a large sauté pan. Place the dumplings in the pan, flat side down. Reduce heat and cook 1 minute or until golden brown on the flat side. Add ½ cup hot water. Cover and steam 5 minutes, or until almost all the water has evaporated. Add the remaining 1 tablespoon oil.
7. Place fried side up on a serving platter, with Dipping Sauce on the side.

DIPPING SAUCE

1 tablespoon soy sauce
2 tablespoons vinegar

1 tablespoon minced fresh
 gingerroot

Combine the ingredients at least 20 minutes before serving.

MANDARIN DELIGHT

HOT AND SOUR SOUP

⅔ cup (approximately) dried
   wood ear mushrooms
⅔ cup (approximately) dried
   black mushrooms
2 teaspoons salt
1 teaspoon sugar
⅓ cup shredded tofu
¼ cup shredded pork loin
2 tablespoons soy sauce

3 tablespoons vinegar
1 teaspoon sesame oil
1 teaspoon black pepper
3 tablespoons cornstarch
5 eggs, lightly beaten
2 tablespoons shredded
   green onion
2 tablespoons shredded
   fresh gingerroot

1. Soak the wood ears and black mushrooms in hot water for 30 minutes or until softened. Cut off the tough stems and shred (you want ⅓ cup of each, shredded).
2. Bring 6 cups water to a boil with the salt and sugar. Add the shredded mushrooms, tofu, pork, soy sauce, vinegar, sesame oil, and black pepper. Stir well, reduce heat, cover, and simmer 5 minutes.
3. Dissolve the cornstarch in 3 tablespoons cold water. Stir into the soup. Turn off the heat. Pour the eggs into the soup in a thin stream, stirring lightly.
4. Stir in the remaining ingredients. Serve.

LEMON CHICKEN

½ cup plus 1 tablespoon
   cornstarch
2 cups flour
1 egg, beaten
   Peanut oil for deep-frying
4 boneless whole chicken
   breasts, skinned

3 tablespoons sugar
1½ teaspoons salt
3 tablespoons fresh lemon
   juice or lemonade
   concentrate
1 lemon, sliced

1. Combine ½ cup cornstarch and flour. Mix in the egg and 2 cups water until smooth and even.
2. Heat the oil in a wok until almost smoking, or about 375°. Dip the chicken breasts in the batter to coat completely. Deep-fry until golden brown. Remove with a slotted spoon.

3. In a saucepan or another wok, heat the sugar, salt, remaining 1 tablespoon cornstarch, and lemon juice with 1 cup water. When thickened, add the lemon slices.

4. Return the chicken breasts to the wok with the oil and deep-fry another 10 seconds. Drain again. Cut into short, 1"-wide strips.

5. Place the chicken on a serving platter. Pour the lemon sauce over and serve.

SZECHUAN SHREDDED BEEF
with Hot Pepper Sauce

½ pound beef flank steak
1 tablespoon soy sauce
1 teaspoon sugar
1 teaspoon chopped fresh gingerroot
1 cup plus 2 tablespoons cooking oil

4 dried red peppers
¼ pound carrots, shredded
1 tablespoon chopped fresh garlic
¼ pound celery, shredded
½ teaspoon sesame oil

1. Cut the flank steak into thin strips across the grain. Cut the strips into thin slices, and shred the slices.

2. Combine the soy sauce, wine, sugar, and ginger. Marinate the shredded beef in the mixture for 30 minutes.

3. Heat 1 cup oil in a wok over high heat. Deep-fry the beef for 3 minutes; remove with a slotted spoon. Remove the oil from the wok.

4. Reheat the wok. Add the remaining 2 tablespoons oil; when hot, add the hot peppers and stir-fry 1 minute. Add the carrots and garlic; stir-fry until the carrots are crisp-tender, about 1½ minutes. Add the celery and beef. Toss lightly to mix. Add the sesame oil and remove to a serving platter.

EIGHT-TREASURE CHICKEN

1 *pound boned raw*
   chicken meat
1 *teaspoon salt*
1 *egg white*
1 *tablespoon plus 1 teaspoon*
   cornstarch
3 *cups oil for deep-frying*
¼ *cup walnuts, chopped*

¼ *cup almonds*
¼ *cup cashews*
¼ *cup sliced mushrooms*
¼ *cup baby corncobs*
¼ *cup diced water chestnuts*
¼ *cup frozen mixed peas*
   and carrots
SEASONING SAUCE

1. Place the chicken meat between 2 sheets of waxed paper. Pound with a meat mallet or the flat of a cleaver to tenderize and flatten. Cut into bite-size pieces.
2. Combine the salt, egg white, 1 tablespoon cornstarch, and ¼ cup water. Add the chicken pieces and marinate at least 20 minutes.
3. Heat the oil to almost smoking in a wok over high heat. Deep-fry the chicken pieces for 30 seconds or until opaque. Remove with a slotted spoon.
4. Remove all but about 2 tablespoons oil from the wok. Return the chicken to the wok and add the remaining ingredients. Stir-fry just until the flavors blend, about 1½ minutes. Remove with the sauce to a serving platter.

SEASONING SAUCE

1 *teaspoon sugar*
2 *tablespoons soy sauce*
1 *tablespoon garlic powder*
1 *tablespoon ground ginger*
1 *tablespoon oyster sauce*

1 *tablespoon rice wine*
½ *cup water*
1 *teaspoon cornstarch*
½ *teaspoon sesame oil*

Combine all ingredients.

KUNG PAO SHRIMP WITH PEANUTS
in Hot Sauce

¾ pound medium-size
  shrimp
1 tablespoon soy sauce
1 teaspoon sherry
1½ tablespoons cornstarch

Peanut oil for deep-frying
6 dried red peppers
SEASONING SAUCE
½ cup peanuts

1. Shell, devein, and thoroughly rinse the shrimp. Combine the soy sauce, sherry, and cornstarch with 1½ tablespoons water. Marinate the shrimp 20 minutes in the mixture.
2. Heat the oil to almost smoking in a wok over high heat. Deep-fry the shrimp 1 minute and remove with a slotted spoon. Remove the oil from the wok.
3. Heat 2 tablespoons oil in the wok. Add the hot peppers and stir-fry about 1 minute. Add the shrimp and Seasoning Sauce and stir gently until the sauce is thickened. Add the peanuts; mix well and remove to a serving platter.

SEASONING SAUCE

1 tablespoon sherry
1 tablespoon soy sauce
½ cup chopped green onion
2 teaspoons sugar

½ teaspoon sesame oil
1 teaspoon cornstarch
1½ tablespoons water

Combine all ingredients.

Navarre's

Dinner for Four

Cracked Crab on Ice with Mustard Sauce

Navarre's Salad

Chicken Livers and Sweetbreads Chasseurs

Rice Pilaf

Cherries Jubilee

Beverages:

With the Dinner—Pouilly-Fuissé

After Dinner—Cognac, Remy Martin

Don Shourds, Owner

Don McLane, Chef

NAVARRE'S

Navarre's owner and manager, Don Shourds, seems to have a gift for remembering names and faces. Perhaps this is due to being in business for over twenty-six years, with bartenders, waiters, and other staff of eighteen to twenty years' service. In any case, he likes to greet repeat clientele by name. "People like to be remembered," he explains. "In this computer age, it's nice to have a personal touch."

Navarre's service is also special, starting with the parking attendant and continuing throughout the evening. One is ushered into a dining room of golds and browns, with a large cherub fountain in the center. Candlelight, crisp linens, and formally dressed waiters create an elegance reflected in the brass light fixtures and the tasteful paintings adorning the walls. Soft music is evident, filtering through from an area containing a large bar with an eye-catching mural portraying a French street scene. The eye-catching quality is partly due to the way the mural follows the contoured wall, lending an appearance of depth to the scene.

Lunches are fairly casual at Navarre's, but elegance is stressed at dinner. Tableside service may be seen when the Rack of Lamb is carved at table, or when Cherries Jubilee is presented for someone special. Well known for double New York steaks and Chateaubriand, the menu is also extremely varied—it has been said that if you can't find something to appeal to you on Navarre's menu, you are just having a bad day.

52 East Camelback
Phoenix

CRACKED CRAB ON ICE
with Mustard Sauce

1 cup mayonnaise
1 cup sour cream
1 cup prepared mustard

2 tablespoons dry mustard
4 cooked Dungeness crabs, split

1. Combine the mayonnaise, sour cream, and both mustards. Place in a glass serving bowl.
2. Cover a serving platter with cracked ice. Place the crabs over, with the mustard sauce in the center.

NAVARRE'S SALAD

1 head iceberg lettuce
½ head romaine lettuce
1 onion, grated
2 tablespoons A-1 sauce
1 cup salad oil
⅓ cup wine vinegar

Salt to taste
½ cup seasoned croutons
8 anchovy filets
Freshly ground black pepper to taste

1. Tear the lettuces into bite-size pieces. Wash and drain thoroughly. Place in a salad bowl.
2. Combine the grated onion, A-1 sauce, salad oil, vinegar, and salt. Place in a cruet.
3. At table, toss the lettuces with the dressing. Add the croutons and toss again. Place on chilled individual salad plates. Top with anchovy filets and freshly ground pepper.

CHICKEN LIVERS AND SWEETBREADS CHASSEURS

4 veal sweetbreads	½ cup chopped green onions
24 chicken livers	½ cup sliced mushrooms
Flour for dredging	2 cups ESPAGNOLE SAUCE
Butter	⅓ cup sherry

1. Soak the sweetbreads in water for at least 5 hours, changing the water several times.
2. Place the sweetbreads in a pan of fresh cold water. Slowly bring to a boil, stirring occasionally. When the membranes appear stiff, drain and rinse under cold water.
3. Peel off the membranes, separating the round lobes from the long ones in the process.
4. Dredge the sweetbreads and chicken livers in flour. Sauté in butter over medium-high to high heat until golden brown.
5. Add the green onions, mushrooms, Espagnole Sauce, and sherry. Stir to heat and serve.

ESPAGNOLE SAUCE

1 onion, diced	2 tablespoons flour
2 stalks celery, diced	2 cups beef stock, hot
1 carrot, diced	Salt and pepper to taste
2 tablespoons butter	

1. Sauté the vegetables in the butter in a heavy sauce pot until the onions are transparent.
2. Stir in the flour. Cook 10 minutes, stirring constantly. Do not allow to burn.
3. Stir in the beef stock until smooth and slightly thickened. Season to taste with salt and pepper. Strain before using.

RICE PILAF

2   tablespoons butter
3   tablespoons finely chopped
    onion
1   cup rice

2   cups Chicken Stock (see
    index)
    Salt and pepper to taste

1. Preheat oven to 350°.
2. Melt the butter over medium-high heat in a saucepan. Add the onion and sauté until transparent.
3. Add the rice and sauté about 5 minutes, stirring frequently.
4. Add the stock and salt and pepper. Cover tightly and bake in preheated oven for 10 to 15 minutes or until all the liquid has been absorbed.

CHERRIES JUBILEE

1   (16-ounce) can pitted
    Bing cherries
3   tablespoons sugar
    Dash of cinnamon

Juice of ½ lemon
2   tablespoons butter
¼   cup cognac, warmed
    French vanilla ice cream

1. Place the cherries with their juice in a sauté pan over medium heat. Cook until bubbling.
2. Add the sugar, cinnamon, and lemon juice. Stir to dissolve and heat briefly.
3. Add the butter. When melted, pour the cognac over the cherries and ignite.
4. Spoon over ice cream in individual dessert dishes.

Dinner for Four

Los Olivos Fresh Lime Margaritas

Nachos

Chimichangas Supreme

Refried Beans

Spanish Rice

Fried Ice Cream

Beverage:

Brisa light or dark, served with a lime wedge

Ruby, Gretchen, Chispa, A.C., Johnny and Hector Coral, Owners

Juanita Recalde, Chef

LOS OLIVOS

Los Olivos is the oldest existing Mexican restaurant in Scottsdale. The Corral family, who emigrated from Mexico in 1919, are now in their second generation at Los Olivos' two restaurants. Before opening the first restaurant, family members worked in the cotton fields; their resting spots were in the shade of the olive trees from which their own "oases" took their name.

Entrance into the colorful, bougainvillea-covered building on Second Street is gained through a beautiful leaded-glass door with olive-tree designs. Inside, both booths and open table arrangements are done in blue and rust shades. Stained-glass windows and, in the cocktail lounge, a unique hand-carved chandelier (by an artist uncle) compete with the artwork on display for the attention of wandering eyes. Strolling musicians offer light entertainment in the dining room, while in a large, separate back room, a Mexican-American band encourages one to join the Latin mood.

Los Olivos is famous for its homemade tortillas, Steak Picado, Carne Asada, and other familiar Mexican foods. The authenticity of the fare is maintained by Juanita Recalde, an old family friend and an excellent cook. If one must wait for a table, one may sit in the cocktail area and contemplate the goldfish in the indoor pond, or have a seat at the bar and sip a cool margarita before dinner.

7328 Second Street, Scottsdale

1300 North Hayden Road, Tempe

LOS OLIVOS FRESH LIME MARGARITAS

1 cup fresh lime juice
Salt
1 cup Cuervo Gold tequila
½ cup triple sec orange liqueur

1 tablespoon sugar
1 tablespoon water
1 egg white
1 quart crushed ice

1. Moisten the rims of 4 (7-ounce) glasses with a little lime juice. Roll the rims in salt to coat. Refrigerate.
2. Mix the sugar with the water. Place in a blender with the tequila, lime juice, triple sec, and egg white. Blend well; add the crushed ice and blend briefly.
3. Pour carefully into the glasses without washing off any of the salt. Add more ice to taste if the drink is too strong.

NACHOS

8 corn tortillas
Oil for deep-frying
*½ pound Wisconsin cheddar
cheese, grated*

*Canned jalapeño peppers,
diced (optional)*
*LOS OLIVOS SALSA
(see next page)*

1. Preheat broiler.
2. Cut the tortillas into wedges. Deep-fry until they rise to the surface of the oil; drain on paper toweling.
3. Place the tortilla chips in a casserole. Sprinkle the grated cheese over and place in preheated broiler for about 2 minutes or until the cheese is melted.
4. Sprinkle with diced jalapeño peppers, if desired. Serve with Los Olivos Salsa.

*Nachos may also be served with sour cream, guacamole, or refried beans.
Try a combination of all of them if you are adventurous!*

LOS OLIVOS SALSA

4 tomatoes, diced
½ onion, diced
2 small fresh jalapeño
    peppers, diced
¼ cup chopped cilantro

1 teaspoon salt
½ teaspoon garlic powder
1 tablespoon vinegar
½ cup tomato purée

Combine all ingredients at least 1 hour before serving; refrigerate if holding longer.

Cilantro is also known as Chinese parsley or fresh coriander.

CHIMICHANGAS SUPREME

1 pound lean beef
1 teaspoon salt
¼ teaspoon pepper
¼ teaspoon garlic powder
4 tomatoes
1½ teaspoons shortening
½ onion, chopped
½ bell pepper, chopped
1½ teaspoons flour
½ cup canned whole green
    chiles

4 flour tortilloas
Oil for deep-frying
RED CHILE SAUCE
1 cup shredded Wisconsin
    cheddar cheese
¼ cup chopped green onions
1 cup sour cream
1 tablespoon whipping cream
GUACAMOLE
2 cups shredded lettuce
4 black olives

1. Cut the beef into 4 pieces. Place in a 5 to 6-quart pan and add water to cover. Bring to a boil; skim the foam from the surface. Add the salt, pepper, and garlic. Simmer until tender, approximately 1½ to 2 hours.
2. Drain the beef, reserving ½ cup of the broth. When the meat is cool, shred. Chop 2 of the tomatoes.
3. Melt the shortening in a pan over medium heat. Add the onion and bell pepper and sauté until tender. Add the flour, whisking until no lumps remain, and cook 2 minutes. Add the shredded beef, reserved broth, chopped tomatoes, and whole chiles. Simmer 15 minutes.

4. Place about ½ cup of the meat mixture in a line down the center of each tortilla. Fold both ends over 1" to 2"; fold one side over the other and roll up in a neat package. Secure with a toothpick.
5. Deep-fry in very hot oil (400°) until crisp and well browned. Drain on paper toweling.
6. Preheat the broiler. Place the chimichangas on an ovenproof platter or in a baking pan. Spoon Red Chile Sauce over liberally. Sprinkle with grated cheese and green onions. Place under broiler until the cheese melts.
7. Combine the sour cream and whipping cream. Slice the remaining 2 tomatoes. Top the chimichangas with the sour cream mixture and Guacamole. Garnish with shredded lettuce, sliced tomato, and olives.

RED CHILE SAUCE

½ cup chili powder	½ teaspoon salt
1½ tablespoons lard	¼ teaspoon garlic powder
1 tablespoon flour	

1. Stir the chili powder into 1 cup water. Allow to soak 1 hour.
2. Melt the lard in a large skillet over medium heat. Add the flour and cook, stirring constantly, for 5 minutes.
3. Add the salt, garlic, and chili/water mixture. Stir until hot and thickened.

One cup of Las Palmas Chile Sauce may be substituted for the chili powder and ½ cup of the water.

GUACAMOLE

3 ripe avocados, diced	½ cup sour cream
1 tomato, chopped	¼ cup cottage cheese
¼ onion, chopped	1½ teaspoons salt
½ cup canned green chiles, chopped	¼ teaspoon garlic powder

Place all ingredients in a deep bowl and mash to desired consistency.

This recipe provides enough guacamole to serve with the Nachos as well as the Chimichangas Supreme.

REFRIED BEANS

½ pound pinto beans, soaked
  overnight

1½ teaspoons salt
¼ cup lard

1. Drain off the water in which the beans were soaked. Place the beans in a 3-quart dutch oven with the salt and 2 quarts water. Bring to a boil, reduce heat, and simmer for 3 hours or until the beans are tender, adding more water as necessary. Allow to cool 30 minutes.
2. Remove 1 cup of the cooking water and reserve. Mash the beans in the remaining water to desired consistency.
3. Melt the lard in a large saucepan over medium heat. Add the beans and cook 30 minutes, stirring frequently. Add the reserved cooking liquid as needed to obtain the proper consistency.

SPANISH RICE

1 tablespoon lard
1 cup rice
½ tomato, chopped
¼ onion, chopped
¼ bell pepper, chopped
½ teaspoon salt

¼ teaspoon pepper
¼ teaspoon garlic powder
2 tablespoons tomato purée
2½ cups Chicken Stock (see
  index)

1. Melt the lard in a 2-quart saucepan over medium heat. Add the rice and brown lightly, stirring constantly.
2. Add the tomato, onion, and bell pepper and fry until tender, stirring often.
3. Add the salt, pepper, garlic powder, tomato purée, and chicken stock. Bring to a rolling boil. Cover, reduce heat, and simmer 20 minutes or until all the liquid is absorbed.

FRIED ICE CREAM

1 quart vanilla ice cream	*Oil for deep-frying*
½ teaspoon ground cinnamon	*¼ cup honey*
½ cup sugar	*Whipped cream*
1 cup cornflake crumbs	*4 maraschino cherries*

1. Let the ice cream stand at room temperature for about 5 minutes to soften slightly.
2. Combine the cinnamon, sugar, and cornflake crumbs in a shallow pan.
3. Using an ice-cream scoop, make 4 large balls of ice cream. Roll these balls in the crumb mixture to cover completely. Wrap in pieces of aluminum foil and freeze for 5 hours.
4. Heat the oil to 450° in a deep pan. As soon as it comes to heat, unwrap the ice-cream balls and deep-fry very briefly—about 2 seconds. Drain momentarily and place in dessert dishes.
5. Top each ball with 1 tablespoon honey, a little whipped cream, and a maraschino cherry. Serve immediately.

The Arizona Biltmore, Phoenix

Dinner for Four

Tartar de Saumon

Soupe d'Escargots en Feuilletage

Salade de Cresson Andalouse

Medaillons de Veau á la Compote d'Oignons

Fraises Jubilee

Wines:

*With the Tartar—Chablis Premier Cru, Joseph Drouhin, 1978, or
Freemark Abbey Chardonnay, 1977*

*With the Veal—Château Trimoulet, St.-Emilion, 1976, or
Spring Mountain Chardonnay, 1978*

*With the Fraises—Perrier-Jouët Champagne, or
Schramsberg Blanc de Blancs*

Siegbert Wendler, Executive Chef

Mark Spelman, Sous-Chef

ORANGERIE

The Orangerie, located in the Arizona Biltmore in Phoenix, is famous for excellence in service and fine Continental dining. The Arizona Biltmore had its grand opening on February 23, 1929, and from that date has been recognized as one of the outstanding landmarks in the state of Arizona. The building itself gives one the feeling of permanence; resort living, elegance, and culture are the principal concepts associated with the Arizona Biltmore.

Upon entering the lobby of the hotel, a cluster of columns, fountains, and plants can be seen just beyond the main doors. Facing the entrance doors across the main lobby is a stained-glass mural designed by Frank Lloyd Wright. At the east end of the lobby is the Orangerie, with its dining room, bar, and cocktail lounge. It is a special, intimate area—part of, yet separated from, the main building. The raised planting area at the entrance has been designed to hold fresh greenery, which thrives indoors and adds to one's first impression. The carpet, with its colorful orange tones and deep coral background, gives the restaurant its name.

Hanging from the high ceiling are the often-mentioned stalactite chandeliers designed by architects of the Frank Lloyd Wright Foundation, complete with mirrored, gold-leafed hexagonal bowls containing foliage. The setting is for an evening of relaxed, fine dining. Glass in the skylight as well as the mirror surfaces seen in the openings of the concrete blocks have been treated with copper to give a soft lavender-gold hue. One has the feeling of dining under the stars.

The restaurant is inviting: tables are set in a grand style, where guests will be received by a charming waiter and assisted by the wine steward. The wine list is presented and resembles in size and weight an old, well-filled family album. The menu is extensive and the food prepared with the utmost care. Tableside cooking is available and very special attention is given to ensure excellent results. The chefs are imaginative and up-to-date on the preparation and presentation of fine foods. *Phoenix* Magazine readers cited the Orangerie as the best restaurant in the valley in 1981; the Orangerie has also won the *Travel/Holiday* Award for Distinctive Dining for the last several years. A final special touch at the restaurant is the handing out of tea roses to the ladies, climaxing an evening of fine gourmet dining.

Arizona Biltmore
Twenty-Fourth Street at Missouri
Phoenix

TARTAR DE SAUMON

Juice of 1 lemon
1 *tablespoon finely chopped fresh dill*
2 *tablespoons finely chopped capers*
1 *teaspoon Grey Poupon mustard*
2 *tablespoons finely chopped onion*
1 *egg, beaten*

2 *tablespoons mayonnaise*
2 *dashes Worcestershire sauce*
Salt and freshly ground black pepper to taste
½ *pound fresh salmon, finely chopped*
Red leaf lettuce
Toast points
Cream cheese

Combine the first 9 ingredients until creamy. Mix the chopped salmon in thoroughly. Line a plate with a leaf of lettuce. Place the salmon mixture over; shape into the form of a fish. Serve with toast points and cream cheese.

SOUPE D'ESCARGOTS EN FEUILLETAGE

¼ *pound plus 2 tablespoons butter*
3 *shallots, finely chopped*
2 *cloves garlic, minced*
6 *mushrooms, finely chopped*
20 *large escargots*
1 *large tomato, peeled, seeded, and diced*
¼ *cup sherry*
2 *cups Chicken Stock (see index)*

1 *teaspoon finely chopped tarragon*
¼ *cup ROUX*
1 *cup whipping cream*
Salt and ground white pepper to taste
½ *pound PUFF PASTRY DOUGH*
1 *egg*
¼ *cup milk*

1. Melt 4 tablespoons butter in a sauce pot over medium heat. Add the shallots and garlic and sauté until transparent. Add the mushrooms, escargots, and tomato. Cover, reduce heat, and simmer about 5 minutes.
2. Remove the cover. Add the sherry and cook until reduced by one-third.
3. Remove the escargots with a slotted spoon and reserve. Add the Chicken Stock and tarragon to the pot. Bring to a boil, add the roux, stirring until thickened and smooth, and remove from the heat.
4. Add the cream slowly while whisking constantly. Add 6 table-spoons butter and whisk until melted and incorporated. Season to taste with salt and white pepper. Return the escargots to the pot. Allow to cool.
5. Preheat oven to 400°.
6. Fill 4 soup cups almost to the rim with the cooked soup. Roll the dough out ⅛" thick and cut into circles to cover the cups.
7. Beat the egg and milk together. Brush the rims of the cups with the wash and cover with the dough circles. Trim the edges if necessary. Cut a small hole in the center of each piece of dough. Brush the dough with the egg wash.
8. Place the cups on a baking sheet and bake in preheated oven for 25 to 30 minutes or until the dough is golden brown. Serve immediately.

ROUX

4 *tablespoons butter*	4 *tablespoons flour*

Melt the butter over medium heat. Stir in the flour and simmer, stirring constantly, for 5 minutes. Do not allow to brown.

PUFF PASTRY DOUGH

1½ *cups sifted flour, plus*	½ *teaspoon salt*
more for rolling	1 *teaspoon baking soda*
½ *pound salted buter*	1 *tablespoon ice-cold water*

Place the flour in a bowl. Make a well in the center; into it place the butter, salt, baking soda, and ice water. Mix by hand until the dough forms walnut-size pieces. Refrigerate until ready to use.

SALADE DE CRESSON ANDALOUSE
Andalusian-Style Watercress Salad

½ *large onion, finely diced*	3 *bunches watercress,*
4 *cloves garlic, minced*	*washed and stemmed*
1½ *teaspoons Dijon mustard*	2 *tomatoes, peeled and cut*
Salt and pepper	*in wedges*
2 *tablespoons red wine*	8 *mushrooms, sliced*
vinegar	2 *tablespoons finely chopped*
¼ *cup sunflower oil*	*fresh basil*

Place the onion, garlic, mustard, salt, pepper, vinegar, and oil in a large bowl; combine thoroughly. Add the watercress, tomatoes, and mushrooms. Toss lightly, taking care not to bruise. Place on chilled individual salad plates and top with basil.

MEDAILLONS DE VEAU A LA COMPOTE D'OIGNONS
Veal Medallions with Stewed Onions

1 *pound veal filet, cut into*
   4 (½"-thick) medallions
Salt and pepper
Flour for dredging
¼ *pound plus 2 tablespoons*
   unsalted butter
½ *cup Madeira wine*
¼ *cup dry white wine*

1¾ *cups whipping cream*
1 *tablespoon julienned*
   Périgord truffle
1½ *pounds onions, finely*
   chopped
1 *tablespoon wine vinegar*
Chopped fresh parsley

1. Season the veal medallions with salt and pepper and dredge lightly in flour. Melt 5 tablespoons butter in a shallow saucepan over medium-high heat. Add the veal and sauté on both sides until lightly browned. Remove to a serving platter and keep warm.

2. Deglaze the pan with the Madeira and white wine, allowing the liquid to reduce to about 3 tablespoons. Reduce heat and add 1½ cups whipping cream. Simmer about 2 minutes or until thickened and smooth. Taste for seasoning and adjust if necessary.

3. Melt 1 tablespoon butter in a separate pan over low heat. Add the truffle and simmer 30 seconds to heat through. Stir into the sauce. Set aside and keep warm.

4. Melt the remaining 4 tablespoons butter in a saucepan with a tight-fitting cover over medium heat. Add the onions, cover, and stew until transparent. Add the vinegar and continue cooking for 5 minutes.

5. Reduce heat to low and slowly stir in the remaining ¼ cup cream. Cook 5 minutes.

6. To serve, place a bed of stewed onions on each plate. Place a veal medallion over and cover with sauce. Garnish with chopped parsley.

FRAISES JUBILEE
Strawberries Jubilee

4 scoops vanilla ice cream	2 tablespoons brandy
4 tablespoons unsalted butter	2 tablespoons Grand
¼ cup granulated sugar	Marnier
2 cups fresh strawberries,	
hulled and quartered	

Place the ice cream in 4 champagne glasses. Keep in the freezer until ready to serve. Melt the butter in a sauté pan over low heat. Add the sugar and stir to dissolve. Add the strawberries and mix well. Add the brandy off the heat; return to heat and ignite the vapors. Repeat to flame the Grand Marnier. Spoon the strawberries and sauce over the ice cream and serve immediately.

Dinner for Six

Mousse de Truite La Reserve

Salade Chicorée aux Lardons Chaud

Noisettes d'Agneau Solognotte

Timbales de Fraises Elysée

Wines:

With the Mousse—Silvaner, Trimbach, 1979

With the Lamb—Moulin à Vent, Louis Latour, 1979

With the Timbales—J. Lohr Select Cluster Chardonnay

Dewey and Patti Beucler, Proprietors

Jacques Gonthier, Executive Chef

LA RESERVE

As one approaches La Reserve, one notices a logo portraying two French country chefs at the entrance to the attached *pâtisserie*. At the same moment, the aromas of freshly baked croissants and pastries assail one's hungry sensibilities. Those who are able to withstand the temptation of immediate gratification then pass an array of antiques and greenery to be greeted by Ariel, the maître d', who turns them over to a well-trained staff of French waiters in formal attire. From this point on, one's every need—and many a mere whim—is attended to.

The green-and-raspberry decor is striking, created by Barbara C. Golden, utilizing Pierre Deux fabrics. Mirrors, candlelight, and soft classical music in the background add a romantic touch. The walls and ceiling are softly padded in complementary fabrics to absorb extraneous noises; tablecloths, lampshades, and assorted accessories are color-coordinated to produce an unusual visual harmony. A large, preserved tree sways gently in the center of the dining room, while copper vases hold fresh flower arrangements. The large mirror behind the oak bar is designed with art-nouveau flair. All in all, this French provincial restaurant creates an elegant feeling.

Executive Chef Jacques Gonthier presides over a team including Sous-Chef Jean-Louis Joubert, Pastry Chef Patric Caillon, and several assistants to prepare a menu for which quality and freshness are considered indispensable. So intent on this principle is Chef Gonthier that he has had the menu to read, "If a dish is missing today from our menu, do not be disappointed. From the market selection, the quality I required was not available." He is certainly qualified to carry out such an ideal: his impressive credentials include the Prix de Maître Cuisinier Prosper Montagne, the Diplomé Taitinger, and the Poêle d'Or 1972, among others.

A unique feature of La Reserve is the wine locker, wherein guests may keep wines purchased from the restaurant's list of moderately priced to very select vintages. The lockers are individually labeled and kept under lock and key at fifty-seven degrees, and the wines are accessible only when the patron has turned his key over to the maître d'. In addition, Ariel looks forward to the wine tastings he coordinates periodically for devotees of the grape.

6166 North Scottsdale Road
Scottsdale

MOUSSE DE TRUITE LA RESERVE

1 (14-ounce) lake trout,
   fileted
1 egg white
½ teaspoon salt
   Pinch of paprika
   Pinch of nutmeg
¼ teaspoon freshly ground
   black pepper

1½ cups whipping cream
12 cooked freshwater crayfish
   or jumbo shrimp
12 PUFF PASTRY MEDALLIONS
   (see next page)
6 slices truffle
   BEURRE BLANC (see next
   page)

1. Preheat oven to 350°.
2. Place the fish filets in a blender with the egg white, salt, paprika, nutmeg, and pepper. Process to a fine paste.
3. Rub the fish paste through a fine sieve into a medium-size bowl. Place the bowl in a larger bowl filled with cracked ice. Work in the cream a few tablespoons at a time with a rubber spatula until light and fluffy.
4. Pour into a buttered mold. Cover and set in a roasting pan; add enough water to come halfway up the side of the mold. Bake in preheated oven for 25 minutes or until a cake tester comes out clean.
5. Unmold onto a warm platter. Garnish with the crayfish or shrimp, pastry medallions, and sliced truffle. Serve with Beurre Blanc.

Brook trout, salmon trout, or the tail end of salmon filet may be substituted for the lake trout if necessary. Américaine or Périgueux sauce are alternatives for the Beurre Blanc. A mortar may be used to grind the fish if a blender is not available.

PUFF PASTRY MEDALLIONS

1 to 2 sheets Puff Pastry Dough
  (see index)

1 egg yolk
1 tablespoon water

Preheat oven to 400°. Using a fish-shaped cookie cutter, cut out 12 medallions from the puff paste. Transfer to a baking sheet. Beat the egg yolk and water together and brush the tops of the medallions with the mixture. Do not allow any to drip down the sides. Bake in preheated oven until puffed and golden, about 12 minutes.

BEURRE BLANC

¼ pound shallots, finely
  chopped
1 cup white wine vinegar
½ cup dry white wine
  Pinch of salt

Freshly ground white
  pepper
½ pound plus 2 tablespoons
  unsalted butter

1. Place the shallots, vinegar, wine, salt, pepper, and ½ cup water in a small, heavy saucepan. Bring to a simmer, partially cover, and cook gently for 1 hour. Strain, reserving the liquid and discarding the shallots.
2. In another small saucepan, bring 1 tablespoon water to a boil over very low heat. Whisk in ¼ pound of the butter, bit by bit. When thickened, add half the shallot liquid and continue to whisk until thoroughly incorporated.
3. Add the remainder of the butter, 2 tablespoons at a time, whisking until incorporated. Whisk in the remainder of the shallot liquid. Taste for seasoning and adjust if necessary.

SALADE CHICORÉE AUX LARDONS CHAUD

1 *American endive, chopped*
Dash of salt
Dash of pepper
¼ *teaspoon red wine vinegar*
2 *cloves garlic, minced*

¼ *pound bacon, cooked*
(fat reserved)
2 *hard-cooked eggs, finely*
chopped
6 *garlic croutons*

1. Preheat oven to 400°.
2. Thoroughly wash the endive three times in cold water. Shake well and drain or spin dry.
3. Place in a clay crock and place in preheated oven for 1 minute. Do not overcook.
4. Crumble the bacon over. Drizzle with the reserved bacon fat. Arrange the eggs and croutons over and serve immediately.

NOISETTES D'AGNEAU SOLOGNOTTE

3 tablespoons butter
3 apples, halved, peeled, and cored
¼ cup sugar
6 small (3") carrots, peeled
6 large mushrooms, washed
12 (3 to 4-ounce) lamb loin medallions
Pinch of salt
Pinch of pepper
1 tablespoon oil
2 cups fresh berries
1 cup cooked wild rice, hot
6 canned artichoke hearts
6 tablespoons Chestnut Creme (see index)
SAUCE PORTO

1. Melt 2 tablespoons butter in a saucepan over medium heat. Add the apple halves and sprinkle with the sugar. Cook 10 to 15 minutes or until tender, stirring frequently to prevent burning. Set aside.

2. Boil the carrots whole until tender, about 8 to 10 minutes. Drain and set aside.

3. Remove the stems of the mushrooms and boil the caps for 3 minutes. Drain and set aside.

4. Sprinkle the lamb medallions with salt and pepper. Melt the remaining 1 tablespoon butter and the oil in a large sauté pan over medium heat. Add the medallions and sauté quickly on both sides. They should be lightly browned on the outside and pink inside. Remove to a serving platter and keep warm.

5. Stuff the cooked apple halves with the fresh berries. Stuff the mushrooms with the hot wild rice. Fill the artichoke hearts with the chestnut creme. Arrange all three and the carrots in an attractive fashion on the lamb platter. Ladle Sauce Porto over the lamb and serve.

Blackberries, blueberries, boysenberries, or red currants are recommended for stuffing the apples. This dish might be served with steamed broccoli or asparagus as a vegetable.

LA RESERVE

SAUCE PORTO

3 tablespoons beef drippings	1 sprig thyme
3 to 4 tablespoons diced fat salt pork or fat bacon	1 bay leaf
1½ carrots, coarsely chopped	1 clove garlic
1 small onion, coarsely chopped	1 quart beef stock, boiling
1 stalk celery, coarsely chopped	⅓ cup rich tomato sauce, or 3 tablespoons tomato concentrate
3 tablespoons flour	6 tablespoons imported port wine
2 sprigs parsley	

1. Melt the beef drippings in a large, heavy saucepan over medium-high heat. Add the diced pork or bacon, carrots, onion, and celery and cook until golden. Sprinkle with the flour, reduce heat to low, and cook, stirring frequently, until well browned.

2. Tie the parsley, thyme, bay leaf, and garlic in a small square of cheesecloth. Add to the simmering vegetables. Add one-third of the boiling stock and cook, stirring, until the sauce thickens.

3. Add half the remaining stock and cook over very low heat, uncovered, for 1½ to 2 hours, stirring occasionally. Periodically skim off the fat and foam that rises to the surface.

4. Stir in the tomato sauce and cook a few minutes longer. Stir through a fine sieve, pressing the vegetables against the sieve to extract all their juices.

5. Clean the saucepan and return the stock to it. Add the remaining stock and cook over low heat until reduced by three-quarters, to about 1¼ cups. Skim the surface occasionally. Allow to cool slightly.

6. Stir in the port. Reheat if necessary before using, but do not allow to boil.

This procedure involves making an Espagnole sauce, reducing it further, and adding the port.

TIMBALES DE FRAISES ELYSÉE

2 *tablespoons unsalted butter, softened*
1 *cup cake flour*
1 *cup confectioners' sugar*
2 *egg whites, stiffly beaten*
2 *tablespoons kirsch*

1 *quart vanilla ice cream*
1 *quart fresh strawberries, hulled and halved*
8 *tablespoons strawberry jam*
1 *cup CRÈME CHANTILLY*

1. Preheat oven to 300°.
2. Rub the butter into the flour. Mix in the sugar, then fold in the egg whites with a rubber spatula. Spread in 8 (5" to 6") rounds as thin as possible on a buttered and floured baking sheet. Bake for 10 to 12 minutes in preheated oven.
3. As soon as the pastry is cool enough to handle, fit each round gently into a cup-shaped dessert glass. Work swiftly; the pastry will lose its flexibility within minutes.
4. Sprinkle with kirsch. Fill each glass with 1 scoop ice cream and ½ cup strawberries. Cover with 1 tablespoon jam. Place the Crème Chantilly in a pastry bag and pipe a decorative ring around each timbale. Serve immediately.

This recipe makes 8 servings. Unused cake rounds will keep, covered, in the refrigerator for a few days. Any other fruit will work in place of the strawberries if desired; the jam should be substituted to complement the fruit.

LA RESERVE

CRÈME CHANTILLY

½ pint whipping cream
1 teaspoon orange flower
water

½ teaspoon vanilla extract
2 tablespoons confectioners'
sugar

Whip the cream in a bowl over ice water, gradually adding the remaining ingredients, until it holds its peaks.

THE PHOENIX HILTON

Dinner for Six

Ragout Fin

Duck Soup à la Minsk

Salad Duke Harrington

Paella Phoenix

Black Raspberries Ambrosia

Wines:

With the Ragout, Soup, and Salad—Puligny-Montrachet

With the Paella—Inglenook Fumé Blanc

With the Ambrosia—Asti Spumante, Cinzano

Horst W. Aschmann, Manager and Maître d'

SANDPAINTER

The Sandpainter in the Phoenix Hilton enjoys a history of culinary excellence begun in 1896 by the Hilton's predecessor, the Adams Hotel. Now, almost a century later on the same site, the Sandpainter continues to offer a luxurious respite from the city, treating diners to gourmet Continental Cuisine.

Entering the Sandpainter, one notices the large sand painting by noted craftsman Ernest Hunt. The dining room is decorated in earth tones, reflecting Arizona's heritage of color. Plum chairs, copper fixtures, panels of brass and glass, and an Indian-inspired copper frieze over the booths are set off by the hues of an Arizona sunset. Soft lighting and sophisticated music round off the edges of an enchanted setting.

The Sandpainter features aged beef, delectable seafood, and impeccable service. Paella, baked goose in a special sauce, and pheasant under glass are proudly recommended for special occasions; tableside cooking is also available with advance notice. Manager and Maître d' Horst Aschmann is pleased to accommodate one's fancies—he even does the tableside cooking himself. A pastry chef bakes on premises twice daily, providing cakes, tortes, pastries, and a variety of assorted specialties. To complement the meal, the wine cellar offers a range of selections from vintners around the world.

Phoenix Hilton
Central and Adams
Phoenix

SANDPAINTER

RAGOUT FIN

¼ pound unsalted butter
¾ pound milk-fed veal,
    deveined and diced
1 cup sliced fresh mushrooms
1 teaspoon tarragon

1 teaspoon diced capers
1 cup white wine
1 tablespoon WHITE ROUX
6 Pepperidge Farm frozen
    puff pastry shells, baked

1. Melt the butter in a large sauté pan over high heat. Add the diced veal, mushrooms, tarragon, and capers and sauté for 4 to 6 minutes.
2. Stir in the wine and, slowly, the roux. Simmer until smooth and creamy.
3. Ladle into the pastry shells and serve.

WHITE ROUX

1 tablespoon butter

1 tablespoon flour

Melt the butter over medium-high heat. Whisk in the flour for 1 minute and remove from heat.

DUCK SOUP A LA MINSK

½ *duck*
4 *carrots*
4 *stalks celery*
3 *bay leaves*
1 *bunch fresh parsley*
½ *teaspoon thyme*
1 *teaspoon tarragon*
1 *medium-size white onion*
2 *cups white wine*

Dash of salt
Dash of white pepper
1 *cup sugar*
Juice of 2 lemons
1 *cup raisins*
2 *medium-size apples,*
  peeled and sliced
GERMAN DUMPLINGS

1. Place the first 11 ingredients in a large stock pot. Add 2 quarts water; bring to a boil, reduce heat, cover, and simmer for 3 hours or until tender, adding more water if necessary to keep the duck covered.
2. Remove the duck from the stock and sieve the stock into a clean pot. Remove the skin, bones, and cartilage from the duck. Dice the dark, lean meat only into the stock. (Retain the remaining meat for other use.)
3. Add the sugar, lemon juice, raisins, and apples to the stock and return to a simmer. Add the dumpling batter by the spoonful. Cook 5 minutes and serve.

GERMAN DUMPLINGS

2 *cups flour*
1 *cup finely diced white bread*
1 *cup milk*
½ *teaspoon white pepper*
½ *teaspoon salt*

1 *teaspoon baking powder*
½ *teaspoon nutmeg*
1 *teaspoon vanilla extract*
3 *eggs, beaten*

Combine all ingredients and mix until smooth. The dough will be of a semi-stiff consistency.

SALAD DUKE HARRINGTON

3 bunches watercress,
   washed
6 hearts of palm, sliced

1 cup chopped walnuts
   DRESSING, hot

Toss together the watercress, hearts of palm, and walnuts. When ready to serve, pour the hot Dressing over.

DRESSING

1 tablespoon chopped
   fresh dill
6 tablespoons olive oil
   Juice of 2 lemons
1 tablespoon sugar
1 tablespoon French mustard

½ teaspoon Tabasco sauce
½ teaspoon tarragon
6 tablespoons white wine
2 tablespoons brandy
   Dash of salt
   Dash of pepper

Combine all ingredients in a saucepan. Bring to a boil and remove from heat.

PAELLA PHOENIX

6 frogs' legs
6 chicken legs
1 pound beef tenderloin, cut in chunks
¾ pound Spanish chorizo, cut in chunks
6 to 8 tablespoons olive oil
2½ cloves garlic, finely chopped
1 tablespoon minced shallots
1 teaspoon tarragon
Salt
Pepper
1 cup chopped onion
2 cups uncooked white rice
4 cups REDUCED CHICKEN STOCK
2 cups white wine
2 tablespoons lemon juice
2 bay leaves
¼ teaspoon saffron
2 teaspoons paprika

½ teaspoon clam base
6 tomatoes
6 tablespoons HARD GARLIC BUTTER (see second page following)
18 medium-size shrimp, shelled and cleaned
3 ounces jalapeño cheese, cut into 6 pieces
12 hard-shell clams, scrubbed
12 mussels, scrubbed
1 pound snapper filet, cut in chunks
1 cup green peas
1 red bell pepper, julienned
6 fresh artichoke hearts, parboiled
Lemon wedges
Drawn butter
Garlic bread

1. Brown the frogs' legs, chicken legs, tenderloin, and chorizo in a pan over high heat with 2 tablespoons olive oil, ½ clove chopped garlic, the shallots, tarragon, and dashes of salt and pepper. Remove from heat and keep warm.

2. Heat the remaining 4 to 6 tablespoons olive oil in a large (16" to 18") skillet over medium-high heat. Add the onion and remaining chopped garlic; sauté for 3 to 4 minutes. Add the rice and sauté until translucent.

3. Add the Reduced Chicken Stock, wine, lemon juice, bay leaves, saffron, paprika, clam base, and ½ teaspoon each salt and pepper. Combine well and taste for seasoning, adjusting if necessary. Bring to a boil, reduce heat to low, cover tightly, and simmer 20 minutes.

4. Preheat oven to 375°.

5. Cut the tops off the tomatoes. Scoop out the seeds. Place 1 table-spoon Hard Garlic Butter in each, followed by 3 shrimp and 1 piece jalapeño cheese.

6. Remove the rice pan from heat. Push or stir the browned frogs' legs, chicken legs, tenderloin, and chorizo into the rice. Insert the clams and mussels, hinges down. Push the stuffed tomatoes halfway into the rice. Lay the snapper, peas, red pepper, and artichoke hearts over. Cover tightly and bake in preheated oven for 20 to 30 minutes, or until the chicken and shellfish are cooked.

7. Serve with lemon wedges, drawn (clarified) butter, and fresh, crusty garlic bread.

REDUCED CHICKEN STOCK

4 pounds stewing chicken	5 large carrots, halved
1 pound chicken wings	3 stalks celery with tops, halved
4 peppercorns	
1 bay leaf	2 large onions, studded with 3 cloves
Pinch of thyme	
6 to 8 green onions, chopped	Salt and pepper to taste

1. Place the chicken in a large stock pot with the peppercorns and 6 quarts water. Bring to a boil over medium heat. Skim the foam from the surface, cover, and reduce heat to simmer. Cook 60 minutes, skimming occasionally.

2. Remove the chicken. Bone, reserving the meat for other use. Return the bones and skin to the pot.

3. Add the remaining ingredients and simmer another 2½ hours. Remove the chicken parts and discard. Strain through a sieve and refrigerate until the fat congeals on the surface.

4. Discard the fat and return the stock to medium heat until reduced by two-thirds.

SANDPAINTER

HARD GARLIC BUTTER

2 cloves garlic
¼ pound unsalted butter, room temperature
1½ teaspoons finely chopped parsley

1½ teaspoons lemon juice
1½ teaspoons Worcestershire sauce
Salt and pepper

Grind the garlic into a fine paste with a mortar and pestle. Mix all ingredients thoroughly with a wooden spoon. Roll into a log shape. Wrap in foil and freeze. When ready to use, slice off the desired amount.

This prepared butter is quite handy to have in the kitchen. You will probably find that you want to double or triple this recipe to have extra on hand.

BLACK RASPBERRIES AMBROSIA

½ pound fresh or frozen
   black raspberries
3 tablespoons sugar
¼ cup lime juice
¼ cup angostura bitters

¼ cup Grand Marnier
¼ cup dark 151° rum
1 teaspoon cinnamon
1 quart vanilla ice cream
   Whipped cream

1. Heat the raspberries, sugar, lime juice, and bitters over medium heat until bubbly, about 5 minutes.
2. Add the Grand Marnier and rum. Ignite and sprinkle the cinnamon into the flame, producing a sparkling effect.
3. Place the ice cream in 6 dessert bowls. Pour the raspberries and sauce over. Garnish with whipped cream and serve immediately.

TRADER VIC'S

Dinner for Four

Rangoon Crab

Bongo Bongo Soup

Hot Spinach Salad

Indonesian Lamb Roast

Trader Vic's Snowball Dessert

Wine:

With the Crab—California Gewürztraminer

With the Lamb—California Zinfandel

Victor Bergeron, Owner

Eric Denk, Manager

TRADER VIC'S

The ever-popular Trader Vic's is located in the bustling Fifth Avenue section of Scottsdale, where tourists join residents in scurrying amidst the shops offering crafts, souvenirs, western wear, and nearly everything else. The building itself is an impressive structure towering above its surroundings like a Polynesian temple. Inside, artifacts such as shark jaws, fishnets, baskets, and Polynesian masks are arranged to create an exotic atmosphere. Hanging from the ceiling is an antique Japanese boat, surrounded by glass floats suspended in netting. All that is missing is the sound of breakers in the near distance, and perhaps a humid tropical breeze.

Specializing in Polynesian food, of course, Trader Vic's also offers a large menu of Continental favorites such as Filet of Sole Florentine, Poached Salmon with Red Caviar, Veal Piccata, and Peppercorn Steak. Manager Eric Denk prides himself on always having fresh seafood available. The restaurant is also justly famous for its tropical—and often exotic—cocktails, some of which arrive at the table with a fresh flower or a sprig of fresh mint.

7111 Fifth Avenue
Scottsdale

RANGOON CRAB

¼ pound crabmeat	1 egg yolk
¼ pound cream cheese	24 wonton wrappers
1 teaspoon A-1 sauce	Oil for deep-frying
⅛ teaspoon garlic powder	Hot mustard
¼ teaspoon salt	Cocktail sauce
⅛ teaspoon white pepper	

1. Chop the crabmeat into small pieces. Blend the cream cheese and A-1 sauce in. Add the garlic powder, salt, pepper, and egg yolk and blend well.
2. Place ½ teaspoon of the filling on each wonton skin. Fold the corners over envelope-style. Moisten the edges of the skin with water and twist to seal.
3. Heat the oil until very hot in a wok or deep pan. Fry the packets a few at a time until delicately browned. Drain on paper toweling. Serve with hot mustard and cocktail sauce on the side.

Wonton skins are available in most produce departments as well as at Oriental markets and specialty shops. They may be purchased fresh or frozen. If they are not available, use egg-roll wrappers: cut into four sections and use as above.

BONGO BONGO SOUP

2 cups milk
1 cup light cream
10 fresh oysters, shucked
   and puréed
½ cup cooked spinach, puréed

2 tablespoons A-1 sauce
⅛ teaspoon garlic salt
Salt and pepper to taste
2 tablespoons cornstarch
½ cup whipping cream,
   whipped

1. Heat the milk and cream almost to a simmer in a 2-quart saucepan.
2. Add the oyster purée, spinach purée, and seasonings. Heat to simmering—do not allow to boil.
3. Dissolve the cornstarch in ¼ cup cold water. Gradually stir this mixture into the soup until the desired consistency is obtained.
4. Ladle into individual soup bowls. Top each with a dollop of whipped cream and glaze under a hot broiler until golden brown.

HOT SPINACH SALAD

2 bunches fresh spinach,
   washed and trimmed
⅔ cup VINAIGRETTE
   DRESSING

¼ cup bacon bits
Freshly ground black
   pepper to taste

Place the spinach in a salad bowl. Heat the dressing in a chafing dish until quite warm; pour over the spinach. Sprinkle the bacon bits over. Finish with several twists of pepper.

VINAIGRETTE DRESSING

7 tablespoons olive oil
3 tablespoons red wine
   vinegar

Juice of ½ lemon
⅛ teaspoon sugar

Mix together thoroughly.

INDONESIAN LAMB ROAST

¾ cup oil	2 dashes Tabasco sauce
⅓ cup finely chopped celery	3 tablespoons honey
⅓ cup finely chopped onion	1 teaspoon oregano
1 clove garlic, minced	2 bay leaves
¼ cup vinegar	½ cup prepared mustard
2 teaspoons A-1 sauce	1 large lemon
3 tablespoons curry powder	1 double rack of lamb

1. Heat the oil in a large saucepan over medium-high heat. Add the celery, onion, and garlic and sauté until the onion is transparent.
2. Stir in the remaining ingredients except the lamb. Bring to a simmer and cook 4 to 5 minutes. Remove from heat and place in the refrigerator to chill.
3. Place the lamb racks in this mixture and marinate in the refrigerator approximately 4 hours, turning several times.
4. Preheat oven to 400°. Drain the lamb, reserving the marinade.
5. Wrap the exposed bones with foil. Place in a greased shallow baking pan and brush with marinade. Bake about 20 minutes or longer, depending on the thickness of the meat and the desired doneness. Turn once while baking; baste often with the marinade.
6. Carve and serve with heated marinade on the side.

TRADER VIC'S SNOWBALL DESSERT

Chocolate sauce or praline sauce	Coconut flakes
Coconut ice cream	

1. Pour the chocolate or praline sauce into the bottom of 4 large scallop shells.
2. Place a generous scoop of coconut ice cream over each.
3. Sprinkle with coconut flakes.

Dinner for Four

Eggs with Black Pearls

Cream of Broccoli Soup

Lobster Salad

Veal with Chanterelles

White Chocolate Mousse Cake

Wines:

With the Meal—A very dry white California wine

With the Dessert—California champagne

Vincent Guerithault, Executive Chef

VINCENT'S

Vincent's is tucked away in the Pinnacle Peak Village complex, just north of Scottsdale. This grouping of shops and stucco buildings with red-tiled roofs is centered around an open courtyard, beautifully landscaped with shrubbery and profusely blooming plants. Benches, chairs, and tables are scattered throughout for those who care to linger in the Arizona sunshine. Just past the Country Store, one notices a charming bakery that appears to have been transported from France. The little shop contains fresh pastries, breads, rolls, and other delicacies baked daily on the premises by chef Vincent Guerithault. Fresh caviar, truffles, raspberry vinegar, and other hard-to-find gourmet items are also seen, as well as jams, jellies, and herbs fresh from Vincent's garden, attractively packaged for gifts or personal use.

But one must get past the bakery to see where the young Chef Guerithault comes into his own. Vincent's dining room is large, with rough plaster walls and Spanish-colonial design. The menu offers classic nouvelle cuisine, from the truffle soup that was one of the first dishes of the genre, to the white chocolate truffle on the dessert list. Chef Guerithault's credentials are stellar: starting at Maxim's in Paris, he was sous-chef at Jean Banchet's internationally praised Le Français in Wheeling, Illinois before being lured to Pinnacle Peak to open the Oaxaca, serving Mexican and French cuisine. Guerithault's abilities soon suggested a different arrangement, and the lower floor of the Oaxaca was converted to a separate restaurant to showcase his inspiration and talent.

Vincent's has drawn praise from New York to California, including a review by Craig Claiborne in the *New York Times* ("exceptional") and a four-page spread in the *Phoenix Home/Garden*. Prior to the rush of notice following Mr. Claiborne's article, Vincent's reputation was primarily word of mouth. Now more and more admirers of fine cooking are willing to make the trip up from Phoenix or beyond. "I invite the public to taste the food I prepare and want it to be a unique dining experience," says Vincent, "with their evening and their money well spent."

8711 East Pinnacle Peak Road
Scottsdale

EGGS WITH BLACK PEARLS

8 eggs	2 tablespoons butter
2 tablespoons cream	1 teaspoon chopped truffle
2 teaspoons chopped parsley	2 ounces caviar
Salt and pepper to taste	Parsley sprigs

1. Neatly cut off the tops of the eggshells; the shells are to be reserved. Lightly beat the eggs with the cream, parsley, salt, and pepper.
2. Melt the butter in a heavy saucepan over low heat. Add the egg mixture and cook, stirring, until slightly thickened.
3. Fill the eggshells halfway with the egg mixture. Divide the chopped truffle over; fill with the remaining egg. Top with the caviar and cover with the shell tops. Stand in attractive glasses and garnish with parsley sprigs.

Eggshells are difficult to cut neatly without the proper tool; however, it is not too hard to break the end off cleanly and not worry about capping the stuffed egg.

CREAM OF BROCCOLI SOUP

1 pound broccoli	1 leek, diced
2 cups whipping cream	Salt and pepper to taste
1½ cups Chicken Stock (see index)	Lemon juice to taste

1. Trim the leaves and thicker stems off the broccoli. Cut in halves or quarters and cook in boiling water until just tender, about 10 to 15 minutes. Drain.
2. Combine the cream and chicken stock in a saucepan. Add the leek and reduce over high heat until the liquid will coat the back of a spoon, about 5 to 10 minutes.
3. Chop the broccoli and combine with the cream mixture. Process in a blender until smooth.
4. Season to taste with salt, pepper, and lemon juice.

LOBSTER SALAD

1¼ pounds lobster tail
Limestone lettuce
Salt and pepper
¼ pound string beans, cooked
¼ pound mushrooms, sliced
¼ pound Belgian endive,
    julienned

1 avocado, sliced
VINAIGRETTE DRESSING
4 large slices black truffle
4 pieces goose liver

1. Steam the lobster tails in their shells for 10 to 12 minutes.
2. While the lobster is steaming, line a salad platter with the lettuce. Salt and pepper the lettuce to taste. Toss the beans, mushrooms, endive, avocado, and Vinaigrette in a bowl and arrange over the lettuce.
3. When the lobster is cooked, drain and shell. Slice into thin medallions and arrange over the salad. Top with the truffle and goose liver.

VINAIGRETTE DRESSING

¼ cup raspberry vinegar   ½ cup hazelnut oil

Place the vinegar in a bowl. Gradually whisk in the oil until thoroughly incorporated.

VEAL WITH CHANTERELLES

1 pound veal loin
Salt
Pepper
Flour for dredging
4 tablespoons butter
¼ pound chanterelle
    mushrooms

2½ teaspoons chopped shallots
1 cup Chablis
2 cups whipping cream
2 cups Reduced Chicken
    Stock (see index)
3 bunches spinach, cooked

1. Slice the veal into 8 equal pieces. Pound to 1" thickness. Season with salt and pepper, then dredge in flour, shaking off any excess.
2. Melt the butter in a saucepan over very high heat. Add the veal and brown; remove from the pan.
3. Add the chanterelles to the same pan and stir until slightly browned. Add the shallots and wine; reduce until dry. Add the cream and stock and reduce until well thickened. Season to taste with salt and pepper.
4. Place the veal on beds of buttered spinach and spoon the sauce over.

WHITE CHOCOLATE MOUSSE CAKE

Makes 8 to 12 servings.

8 *eggs, room temperature*	2 *pounds white chocolate*
1 *cup plus 2 tablespoons sugar*	1 *quart whipping cream, heated*
1 *cup plus 2 tablespoons flour*	*Shaved dark chocolate for decorating (optional)*
4 *tablespoons butter, melted*	

1. Preheat oven to 250°.
2. Whip the eggs with the sugar until creamy. Gently fold in the flour and melted butter.
3. Pour the batter into a greased baking pan about 18" by 26" by 1" deep; the batter should thinly cover the bottom of the pan. Bake in preheated oven for 30 minutes. Allow to cool to room temperature.
4. Break the white chocolate into small pieces and place in a large bowl. Pour the hot cream over and stir until smooth. Place in a larger bowl lined with cracked ice; when cool, whip until thick and fluffy.
5. Cut the cooled sponge cake into long strips, 3" to 4" wide. Assemble by alternating layers of cake and mousse. Cover the top and sides with the remaining mousse. Decorate the sides with shaved dark chocolate, if desired.

THE WIGWAM

Dinner for Six

Melon Appetizer

Gazpacho Salad

Crabmeat Enchiladas

Peanut Butter Cream Pie

Wine:

Robert Mondavi Chenin Blanc

Goodyear Tire and Rubber Company, Owners

William T. McAdams, Executive Chef

THE WIGWAM'S TERRACE DINING ROOM

The Terrace Dining Room at the Wigwam Country Club Resort is located in Litchfield Park, fifteen miles west of Phoenix. The Wigwam is an outgrowth of a Goodyear Tire and Rubber company cotton plantation begun in 1917. The rapid expansion of agricultural activities required a facility to house and attend to the needs of visiting sales representatives and executives. Thus the Organization House came into being—the nucleus unit of what would ultimately evolve into one of the Southwest's most luxurious resorts. The Wigwam opened Thanksgiving Day, 1929 to become a cozy hideaway for winter visitors interested in Western elegance and good food, as well as golf, tennis, swimming, horseback riding, skeetshooting, lawn sports, or even a desert steak-fry.

The Terrace Dining Room is decorated in salmon and blue, with massive wrought-iron chandeliers commanding attention. The cuisine is described as "country cooking—good food prepared simply." A typical menu's entrées range from prime rib au jus through a breaded veal cutlet with spaghetti Milanaise to French pancakes or a seafood of the day. Rolls and pastries are made on premises in the Wigwam Bake Shop; desserts, including pies, cakes, and eclairs, are made by the pastry chef.

The menus change daily, but not the staff nor the service. Many of the staff have been with the Terrace for at least twenty years, providing a continuity and an intuitive sense of decorum unequaled in many establishments.

Wigwam Country Club Resort
Litchfield Park

THE WIGWAM'S TERRACE DINING ROOM

MELON APPETIZER

½ cantaloupe
½ honeydew melon
½ cranshaw melon

1½ cups ginger ale
6 fresh mint sprigs
6 fresh strawberries

1. With a melon baller, scoop the pulp from the melons. Place in a bowl and refrigerate until serving time.
2. Place the melon balls in sherbet dishes. Pour ¼ cup ginger ale over each; garnish with a mint sprig and a fresh strawberry.

GAZPACHO SALAD

2 stalks celery
1 small zucchini squash
1 small cucumber
1 small white onion
1 green bell pepper
1 medium-size carrot

2 tomatoes
1 cup cherry peppers
GAZPACHO MARINADE
Lettuce leaves
6 black olives

Slice the celery on the diagonal in bite-size pieces. Slice the remaining vegetables approximately ¼" thick. Toss together in a bowl and cover with marinade. Refrigerate at least 1 hour. Serve on lettuce-lined salad plates; garnish with black olives.

GAZPACHO MARINADE

¼ teaspoon oregano
2 teaspoons sugar
1 teaspoon salt
1¼ teaspoons garlic salt
1 teaspoon dry mustard
1 cup wine vinegar

1 cup tomato juice
¼ cup light vegetable oil
¼ teaspoon black pepper
1 teaspoon celery salt
8 drops Tabasco sauce
1 cup water

Thoroughly combine all ingredients.

THE WIGWAM'S TERRACE DINING ROOM

CRABMEAT ENCHILADAS

6 corn tortillas
Oil or lard for frying
1½ cups crabmeat
2 tablespoons butter
6 tablespoons minced onion
SALSA CON TOMATILLOS
(see next page)

1½ to 2 cups shredded Jack cheese
SOUR CREAM SAUCE (see next page)
Pitted ripe olives
Avocado slices
Tomatoes, peeled and sliced

1. Preheat oven to 400°.
2. Fry the tortillas in oil or lard until soft; drain on paper toweling.
3. Sauté the crabmeat in the butter until hot. Place ¼ cup in the center of each tortilla. Top with 1 tablespoon minced onion and a little Salsa con Tomatillos. Roll up the tortillas and place in a shallow baking pan.
4. Cover with the remaining Salsa. Sprinkle generously with shredded cheese and bake in preheated oven about 10 minutes or until hot and the cheese is melted.
5. Serve with a dollop of Sour Cream Sauce. Garnish with olives, avocado slices, and tomato slices.

Be sure all the prep work is done before you begin working. When working with tortillas, they must be rolled quickly or they will become dry.

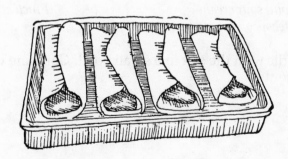

THE WIGWAM'S TERRACE DINING ROOM

SALSA CON TOMATILLOS

2 (10-ounce) cans tomatillos
2 corn tortillas
½ cup oil or lard
1 clove garlic
1 tablespoon salt
2 fresh jalapeño or canned
    Ortega chiles, chopped

½ cup chopped onion
1 teaspoon ground cumin
1 teaspoon oregano
Pinch of sugar
1 to 2 drops green food coloring
    (optional)

1. Press the tomatillos and juice through a sieve. Set aside.
2. Fry the tortillas in the oil, one at a time, until crisp and lightly browned. Drain on paper toweling.
3. Mash the garlic clove with the salt in a small bowl. Reheat the tortilla oil in a saucepan over medium heat. Add the chiles and onion and cook until soft but not brown. Add the sieved tomatillos, garlic and salt, cumin, oregano, and sugar. Cook 5 minutes.
4. Crumble the tortillas into the mixture. Place in a blender and process until smooth. Return to the saucepan. Stir in the food coloring if desired. Keep warm until ready to use.

SOUR CREAM SAUCE

¼ teaspoon fresh garlic
½ teaspoon salt
½ pint sour cream
½ teaspoon oregano

½ teaspoon cumin
2 tablespoons chopped onion
Pinch of sugar

Mix the garlic with the salt in a small bowl. Combine with the remaining ingredients.

PEANUT BUTTER CREAM PIE

4 tablespoons butter
2 cups milk
⅓ cup sugar
½ teaspoon salt
¼ cup cornstarch

4 egg yolks
3 tablespoons peanut butter
1 baked 9" pie shell
Whipped cream
Chopped peanuts

1. Bring the butter, milk, sugar, and salt to a boil.
2. Mix the cornstarch in ½ cup cold water. Mix in the egg yolks. Whisk into the boiling milk mixture until thick.
3. Remove from heat and whisk in the peanut butter. Pour into the pie shell. Allow to cool before topping with whipped cream. Garnish with chopped peanuts.

Appetizers

Beverages

Breads and Doughs

Desserts and Dessert Accents

RECIPE INDEX

Entrées

THE GREAT CHEFS SERIES
A Collection of Gourmet Recipes from the Finest Chefs in the Country

Each book contains gourmet recipes for complete meals from the chefs of 21 great restaurants.

___ *Dining In–Baltimore*	$7.95	___ *Dining In–Philadelphia*	$8.95
___ *Dining In–Boston*	7.95	___ *Dining In–Phoenix*	8.95
___ *Dining In–Chicago, Vol. II*	8.95	___ *Dining In–Pittsburgh*	7.95
___ *Dining In–Cleveland*	8.95	___ *Dining In–Portland*	7.95
___ *Dining In–Dallas*	7.95	___ *Dining In–St. Louis*	7.95
___ *Dining In–Denver*	7.95	___ *Dining In–San Francisco*	7.95
___ *Dining In–Hawaii*	7.95	___ *Dining In–Seattle, Vol. II*	7.95
___ *Dining In–Houston, Vol. I*	7.95	___ *Dining In–Seattle, Vol. III*	8.95
___ *Dining In–Houston, Vol. II*	7.95	___ *Dining In–Sun Valley*	7.95
___ *Dining In–Kansas City*	7.95	___ *Dining In–Toronto*	7.95
___ *Dining In–Los Angeles*	7.95	___ *Dining In–Vancouver, B.C.*	8.95
___ *Dining In–Manhattan*	8.95	___ *Dining In–Washington, D.C.*	8.95
___ *Dining In–Milwaukee*	7.95	___ *Feasting In Atlanta*	7.95
___ *Dining In–Minneapolis/St. Paul*	7.95	___ *Feasting In New Orleans*	7.95
___ *Dining In–Monterey Peninsula*	7.95		

☐ CHECK HERE IF YOU WOULD LIKE TO HAVE A
DIFFERENT DINING IN–COOKBOOK SENT TO YOU
ONCE A MONTH

Payable by MasterCard, Visa, or C.O.D. Returnable if not satisfied.
List price plus $1.00 postage and handling for each book.

BILL TO: **SHIP TO:**

Name _____   Name _____

Address _____   Address _____

City _____ State ____ Zip _____   City _____ State ____ Zip _____

☐ Payment enclosed   ☐ Send C.O.D.   ☐ Charge

Visa # _____ Exp. Date _____

MasterCard # _____ Exp. Date _____

Signature _____

PEANUT BUTTER PUBLISHING
2445 76th Avenue S.E. • Mercer Island, WA 98040
(206) 236-1982

THE GREAT CHEFS SERIES
A Collection of Gourmet Recipes from the Finest Chefs in the Country

Each book contains gourmet recipes for complete meals from the chefs of 21 great restaurants.

____ *Dining In–Baltimore*	$7.95	____ *Dining In–Philadelphia*	$8.95
____ *Dining In–Boston*	7.95	____ *Dining In–Phoenix*	8.95
____ *Dining In–Chicago, Vol. II*	8.95	____ *Dining In–Pittsburgh*	7.95
____ *Dining In–Cleveland*	8.95	____ *Dining In–Portland*	7.95
____ *Dining In–Dallas*	7.95	____ *Dining In–St. Louis*	7.95
____ *Dining In–Denver*	7.95	____ *Dining In–San Francisco*	7.95
____ *Dining In–Hawaii*	7.95	____ *Dining In–Seattle, Vol. II*	7.95
____ *Dining In–Houston, Vol. I*	7.95	____ *Dining In–Seattle, Vol. III*	8.95
____ *Dining In–Houston, Vol. II*	7.95	____ *Dining In–Sun Valley*	7.95
____ *Dining In–Kansas City*	7.95	____ *Dining In–Toronto*	7.95
____ *Dining In–Los Angeles*	7.95	____ *Dining In–Vancouver, B.C.*	8.95
____ *Dining In–Manhattan*	8.95	____ *Dining In–Washington, D.C.*	8.95
____ *Dining In–Milwaukee*	7.95	____ *Feasting In Atlanta*	7.95
____ *Dining In–Minneapolis/St. Paul*	7.95	____ *Feasting In New Orleans*	7.95
____ *Dining In–Monterey Peninsula*	7.95		

☐ CHECK HERE IF YOU WOULD LIKE TO HAVE A
DIFFERENT DINING IN–COOKBOOK SENT TO YOU
ONCE A MONTH

Payable by MasterCard, Visa, or C.O.D. Returnable if not satisfied.
List price plus $1.00 postage and handling for each book.

BILL TO: **SHIP TO:**

Name _____   Name _____

Address _____   Address _____

City _____ State ____ Zip _____   City _____ State ____ Zip _____

☐ Payment enclosed   ☐ Send C.O.D.   ☐ Charge

Visa # _____ Exp. Date _____

MasterCard # _____ Exp. Date _____

Signature _____

PEANUT BUTTER PUBLISHING
2445 76th Avenue S.E. • Mercer Island, WA 98040
(206) 236-1982

PHO 682